DARE
TO BE
GREAT

DARE
TO BE
GREAT

Unlock
Your Power
to Create a
Better World

POLLY HIGGINS

FL◈NT

A share of the royalties from the sales of the book will go to Ecological Defence Integrity to fund their work to stop ecocide.

First published 2014 by Clink Street Publishing as *I Dare You to be Great*
This updated edition published 2020

FLINT is an imprint of The History Press
97 St George's Place, Cheltenham,
Gloucestershire, GL50 3QB
www.flintbooks.co.uk

British Library Cataloguing in Publication Data.
A catalogue record for this book is available from the British Library.

ISBN 978 0 7509 9410 1

Typesetting and origination by The History Press
Printed by Ashley House Printing Company

TO ALL WHO CARE

My book is written for you; it is my exploration of what it is to dare to be great.

You have here in your hands some keys, some tools and some alchemy discovered along the route of my quest to help you as you set out on yours.

CONTENTS

PRAISE FOR POLLY HIGGINS AND *DARE TO BE GREAT*

Polly is of course known for her work on Ecocide Law; a parallel piece of work was to make it her business to encourage everyone to be their best possible selves. This she did for me and it made the world of difference to be so encouraged, especially by a fellow mischief maker. A way to tune into this encouragement and guidance is to read this book.

She was a dear friend and major personal inspiration in my life, and her attitude to the law was unlike anyone else's. She was creative with it. She saw the potential of law to provoke fundamental societal change, both by shining a light on where it fell short and by directly pushing the envelope.

In her last months she jokingly acknowledged how XR had helped her own work on ecocide become more visible, saying, 'I love Extinction Rebellion! They make us look moderate.' And if we have brought the possibility of criminalising ecocide closer, we are doing our job.

Dr Gail Bradbrook, co-founder of Extinction Rebellion

A great spirit speaks through this book. The late and much beloved Polly Higgins was indomitable, unshakable in her service to the healing of Earth, no stranger to the horrors endured by people and planet, yet consistently positive, cheerful, and inspiring. *Dare To Be Great* embodies all these qualities; what's more, it reveals something of their source and will awaken them in the reader. This book is a potent antidote to burnout and despair, confirming the heart's knowledge that yes, we can do this.

Charles Eisenstein, teacher, speaker and author

Establishing the Law of Ecocide would signal a major breakthrough in the way we deal with crimes against the natural world. Polly Higgins' groundbreaking proposal to list ecocide as the fifth global crime against peace would go a long way towards deterring and holding to account CEOs, companies and nations. Whether it's oil drilling in the Arctic, deforestation in the Amazon, or over-fishing in the Atlantic, activities which impact severely on global ecosystems would be brought under far closer scrutiny. It could also play a significant role in encouraging companies to drop the dirty, polluting industries of old, and invest in the clean technologies and renewable energy solutions of the future.

Caroline Lucas MP, former Leader of the Green Party of England and Wales

I open this book. Again. I hear her voice. I revisit these words, stories, instructions, opinions and invitations. And I ask her out loud what do you mean by this title *Dare To Be Great*?

The synonyms for 'daring' include fearless and foolhardy. Reckless and smart. Game and rash. There is no daring without danger. There is a cost in daring. There is a rebelliousness.

And what is great? A word that has also so many terrible associations. Make ... Great ... again. Delusions of empire. Human grandiosity. So the use of this word is, as is typical for Polly Higgins, 'daring' and dangerous in itself.

Read it. And as you read it through, you will begin to see the appeal, dare I say, the summons she is making with this title ... the summons, the demand, the invitation of this book is simply ... to change. To change ourselves, yes, but also to dare to leave our skins and recognise that we are all part of nature. Which we cannot escape. Just as we cannot escape the planet. In these times that is dangerous possibly, demanding certainly, but perhaps the most creative act we can do. To step daringly out of ourselves into a greater world.

Simon McBurney OBE, actor, writer and director

Polly Higgins gave up her job and sold her house in order to found a campaign on behalf of all of us. She drafted model laws to show what the crime of ecocide would look like, published books on the subject and, often against furious opposition, presented her proposals at international meetings.

I believe establishing such a law would change everything. It would radically shift the balance of power, forcing anyone contemplating large-scale vandalism to ask themselves: 'Will I end up in the international criminal court for this?' It could make the difference between a habitable and an uninhabitable planet.

Polly started something she intuitively knew would continue beyond her own life. It could, with our support, do for all life on Earth what the criminalisation of genocide has done for vulnerable minorities: provide protection where none existed before. Let us make it her legacy.

George Monbiot, journalist, environmentalist and author

FOREWORD

by Marianne Williamson

I didn't have the good fortune of meeting Polly Higgins during her time on Earth, yet her life force comes across strongly in the pages of this book. The Earth she loved so much is better off now, having been graced by her profound compassion and protective spirit. She felt passionately the woundedness of the Earth, and dedicated her life and career to coming to its aid. Now, after her death, the entire world is catching up with her.

I feel a strong connection to Polly because her path was one with which I can identify. What are the internal changes that we have to go through, particularly as women, in order to show up most fully in life? What is the potential we've been trained to keep unrealised, at the cost of giving our gifts to the world? What are the keys to dismantling habits by which we resist our greatness, and thus the part we might otherwise play in the healing of a wounded planet?

I understand the abandonment and betrayal Polly felt when her ideas were too big, too radical, too outrageous – all appropriately so, in order to get the job done – for those around her. I understand the pain she would have had to go through in order to mine the gold of her own internal nature and find the strength to keep on keeping on at a time when she was little understood. I understand how her passionate and total dedication to life gave her the strength she needed to face death unafraid.

Polly Higgins did something extremely important. She changed the way our civilisation looks at the rights of the Earth itself. By bringing the notion of ecocide into legal question, she has expanded the way we think of what is happening around us. Most importantly, as is evidenced by this book, she has guided us to the internal as well as external changes that will change us, and the Earth, enough for humanity to survive. Her illuminating and inspiring insights into the nature of personal evolution display a compassion for people as great as her compassion for the planet on which we live.

In her final words written to those who loved her, Polly made clear her belief that she knew life goes on beyond the life of the body. When it does, the gifts that were given while we were on the Earth remain to grace it. In no one's life is that truer than in the life of Polly Higgins. The Earth literally has a greater chance of survival because of the work she did on its behalf.

To read her words is to be more than inspired; it's also to be humbled. It's impossible to read of her accomplishments and not ask if we ourselves are doing quite enough. If her message is anything, it's that what she did we can do. Where she was great, we can be great. And if we strive for exactly that, I think we'll be blessed as I believe with all my heart that she is blessed, and now living in the joy of God.

Marianne Williamson
February 2020

INTRODUCTION

by Jojo Mehta

This book is a highly unconventional combination of global crusade with personal exploration and discovery, at once deadly serious and irrepressibly playful. In other words, it's probably the closest thing you'll get to a conversation with Polly.

Polly was a lawyer. Her own daring was profoundly grounded in the field she had chosen. She came to law not as an undergraduate nudged by family or school, but as a mature student with two previous degrees. She paid her own way through law school and distinguished herself rapidly as a talented barrister. Her moment of epiphany, 'the Earth needs a good lawyer', had as its unspoken corollary, 'and I am a good lawyer'. Her mission to answer the question, 'How do we create a legal duty of care for the Earth?' was fundamentally premised on her existing expertise. It was uniquely daring: she drafted a definition of a law that would criminalise the destruction of nature – **ecocide** – and submitted it to the UN Law Commission, embarking on a lifelong quest to establish it as a crime at the International Criminal Court.

The book you are now reading arose out of her recognition that we all have the potential to combine our talents with the difference we want to make in the world in creative and impactful ways, if only we have the courage and imagination to do so: 'The greatness lies in self-discernment; where best to put my skills? One good indicator is whether others can step in instead. Ask yourself, who else is creating a new space with the work I am doing? If the answer is none, or very few, then you are being invited to help create the new path.'

Polly had a knack for catalysing change in people – for making them feel completely safe while subtly adjusting their view of the world and increasing their confidence to engage with it. Her indomitable spirit, good humour and sheer charm in the face of what many considered an impossible task, as well as her determined encouragement of others to find their own strength and commitment, fill this book by the bucketload and are a delight to read. (And I challenge anyone to come out of the Earth-care section unconvinced of the absolutely necessity of making ecocide an international crime.)

What is perhaps less obvious on the surface of these pages is what Polly's husband describes as the 'ruthlessness' with which Polly pursued her quest. For her, everything was in service to the single purpose of putting in place a law of ecocide. There was no such thing as a 'day off' in Polly's world, because she lived and breathed her work. There was often a fierce kind of joy in that: she didn't see it as work but as life, and as an adventure. I was her closest colleague and friend during the last four and half years of her life, and it was never less than exhilarating. Truly dedicating your life to a single purpose has a powerful magnetism, and when your unique purpose is protecting the planet – arguably the biggest game in town – that's doubly powerful.

It meant she refused to compromise her vision, and it meant she went without a salary for almost a decade because only a few enlightened individuals were brave enough to back her, and there was never a penny to spare outside the immediate requirements of the work. NGOs and grant-giving foundations considered it too much of a risk, or else wanted milestones and projections she was unable to provide by the very nature of sailing in uncharted waters.

Her dedication to and identification with her mission were relentless and took their toll. There were times of deep despair and doubt when she felt there was no hope of Ecocide Law becoming reality, and because she knew what that would mean, she deeply felt the attendant pain of what would happen to the Earth. Only those very close to her saw those moments, because her face to the world was always cheerful; she had an intuitive understanding that if she was to convince that world, she could not let her own upbeat conviction publicly waver, even for a second.

Her commitment left no room whatsoever for self-pity and gave her a remarkable perspective on the terminal cancer diagnosis she received in March 2019. Unafraid for herself, and pragmatic to the end, she smiled somewhat ruefully and said: 'Shame I have to be on death's door to get attention. But if this is what it takes to get this work off the ground, let's use it.'

In the light of this, a word of caution to the reader: the concept of freedom runs like a golden thread through the text of this book, because much of Polly's own journey was about freeing herself from constraints: the emotional scars of a difficult childhood, the isolation of long periods of hospitalisation with asthma as an adolescent, the stifling expectations of a traditional Catholic upbringing, the adversarial framework of the courtroom. And yet her own need for freedom was subsumed into the greater need she perceived around her – the need of the Earth for a good lawyer. In the end, she didn't get to see the world from the seat of a Harley Davidson, which was her personal dream of freedom, because she had dedicated herself to a bigger dream.

What she shows us beyond the shadow of a doubt, however, is what we can accomplish when we step into our own unique greatness, with authenticity, grounded in our skills and trusting in our intuition, and with a willingness to take risks in service to something beyond ourselves. She had a profound belief in human potential, in the spirit of community and particularly in the spirit of rebellion. She was delighted, in the last week of her life, to see the call to 'Stop Ecocide' taken up on the streets of London during the Extinction Rebellion of April 2019. She understood – correctly – that the seed had been sown and would now take root ...

The year following her death has been nothing short of extraordinary. Far from dying with her, Polly's work has grown beyond anything we imagined a year ago. The NGO we founded together (Ecological Defence Integrity) is working with a team of diplomats, lawyers and research experts taking forward the core legal and diplomatic advocacy work at the international level. We were thrilled when in December 2019 two sovereign states members of the International Criminal Court (Vanuatu and the Maldives) dared to be great and officially called for the Assembly to consider adding a crime of ecocide to the Rome Statute.

Meanwhile the Stop Ecocide campaign has representation in a growing number of countries, raising public awareness and gathering Earth Protectors to support the cause. And more daring still, a pilot scheme for Earth Protector Communities is already under way, seeding a global collaborative movement in which towns, schools and colleges, businesses and other institutions work together to protect land, wildlife, air, soil and water, in anticipation of the eventual adoption of Ecocide Law.

A few weeks after her death, Polly's husband Ian discovered a document on her laptop written at the time of the original publication of *I Dare You to be Great* in 2014, around the time I started working with her. It was simply titled 'I Know'. It was a clear premonition of an early departure, with instructions to be read at the celebration of her life – which she specified was to be a huge party with food, music and dancing. The full text is reproduced at the end of this book, but one phrase belongs here. Polly wrote: 'I know my work is done when others start to call in greatness too.'

This book is your invitation to do so.

Jojo Mehta
February 2020

www.EcocideLaw.com
www.StopEcocide.earth
www.EarthProtectorCommunities.net

PREFACE

This is a book to scribble on and share; it's a book that is a seed and a book to change your life. It comes with a good-health warning: your vision of what is – and what can be – shall alter radically. Let the seed grow within you and feed it liberally. You'll find windows suddenly open, a gust of fresh thoughts and ideas blows in, and new paths emerge to take you forward.

Ours is the journey of the questor. Make no mistake, this quest is participatory. At each juncture you will find keys denoted for you to turn: keys that open up questions for the questor to answer, visions to be brought into being and treasure to be found within. Keys are to be found throughout the book.

Part Two offers up another layer of tools to be added into your repertoire, there to pull out when required. And Part Three adds yet another layer: the alchemy – mine and yours. Each culture has their stories of greatness – what do we choose to be our stories? Not his stories (history), or her stories, but our stories. You'll find here a few of mine, and I am sure you shall have many more that are yours.

Setting out on a quest of greatness calls for a compass, a map and a treasure trove. Only for this quest, the compass is your inner guide, your map is yours for the making and the treasure – well, only you can determine that!

My book is an invitation to you to see the crossroads and take a different path, engage in a different kind of life. This is the book I wish I'd had when I was lost and felt I had no idea where to turn. This book gives hope when there seems to be none and it's an invitation to live a life in service to something so much greater than the self.

So, what is your vision? Dream big. This book is not a step-by-step plan. It is in part a record of my story and my quest, and in part a gift to you so that your quest can be fast-tracked. Bring forth your vision of a more beautiful world. My story is just a carrier, a bridge if you will, to provide a crossing as you step into your greatness. And my way is not the only way – but it could be a good starting point. Please feel free to vary the route map as you go.

PROLOGUE

The Devil On My Shoulder Grinned

A day that changed my life: my birthday, 4 July. Not like any other day: no emails, no writing, nothing except walking in the New Forest in southern England. Soft rain, loads of it. Shoes off, squelching mud and dripping wet. I am happy. It was as if I had become part of the woodland itself.

'What next?' A Law of Ecocide – an international crime to prohibit mass damage and destruction – was so much part of me that I lived and breathed it. I knew that the day would come when I could ask what next. Bizarrely, I found myself asking it on my birthday. A thought popped into my head that took my breath away: 'Dare to be great.'

Yikes. The last time I had asked a big open question that changed my life was seven years earlier. The question then was, 'How do we create a legal duty of care for the Earth?' I had no idea of the journey that would take me on, nor what would come of seeking the answer and yes, I can now say, it has and continues to be a truly great journey that has led me to creating an Earth Law. That was a big question to answer, but this time round I had an answer that came boomeranging in within seconds. An answer that called on me to dare to be great. How on earth do I meet this?

But. There's other work to do – getting a Law of Ecocide into place, for starters. The thing was, if I was to dare to be great, it seemed to me, I'd need to go public with the idea. What? Let people know what I'm thinking and say I'm daring to be great – the devil on my shoulder grinned. I have so much else to do. Or do I? That's the thing with a big idea – once it's out there it has a habit of resurfacing when you least expect it, as if a nudge is required to say, 'What about the big idea?'

Push a good idea down and it has a habit of popping up again in the most unlikely of places. In public. So, I outed myself, not knowing what I would say. I hadn't meant to, but it just popped out. My heart pounded and I just knew I had to do it – it was the unknown territory that put the heebie-jeebies up me.

I'm getting another nudge from the Universe – this is not meant to be a solo flight for just me. Like birds, it's so much easier to fly together. We give each other support as we go. So, come, join me – I dare you to be great too. Then go dare others you meet to be great too. Together, not separate: this is one great adventure to be shared by all.

Polly Higgins,
Summer 2014

P.S. Greatness brings with it a challenge: stay safe and play safe or be open to a very different kind of adventure. It's not about feeling better – it's about getting better at feeling what it is to be truly alive. I can honestly say that when you dare to be great, your life will never be dull.

PART ONE

STEPPING INTO GREATNESS

WHAT IS GREATNESS?

Where do I buy greatness? The thing is, greatness is not something that can be bought – it's a state of being. I can't put in an order on the internet for next-day delivery, to be returned if it doesn't fit. I can't steal it, nor can it be robbed from me. I can't get the size of it, nor can it be weighed.

It's intangible – it's a soul quality. Greatness is inherent in each and every one of us from the very moment we take our first breath as humans newly entered into this strange and wonderful land called Earth. Greatness is a predilection for life itself plus a willingness to give of the self in service to something greater than all of life.

Greatness is not so easy to define, but when we are in the presence of someone great we know it. Somehow, greatness has an energetic pull all of its own – and we can sense it to some degree. That's why some people are publicly fêted, but then for every great person in the public light, there are thousands who are equally great without the public knowing it. Those who are not seen have chosen to go about their work quietly. It is all about choice; neither path is better or worse, indeed there is no better or worse – there are just different avenues that can be taken. The choice is yours. It is the 'why' that determines the greatness. Why do you choose to be a public figure? Is it because you are in service to something greater than yourself, or is it because you want to enjoy fame per se? One is true greatness, the other is an aspiration built on a fear of not being valued. Let go of our fear and we can move forward without compromising our own way of being.

Every day we are challenged to some degree by our own fears; can we truly stand tall and claim, 'I have no fear'? When we have no fear of, say, being undervalued, being taken for granted, being marginalised or ignored, or – worse – being abandoned then the brakes on our lives are released. Fear is one of the most crippling negative energies in the world; fear can, and has, triggered wars, death and destruction. Remove fear from your own life and you are able to function from a very different place, from a place that is driven by positive energy – joy, happiness, peace and, ultimately, love.

This is a tall order – but then again, if we are to dare to be great, then our challenge is indeed great. It is a challenge worthy of being met, and as all adventurers know, the quest ahead will call on our soul qualities, skills and commitment. We can each be great within our lives – if we choose to.

And, if not, in effect you experience something else; what that may be shall inevitably play out, but it may not be of your own choice. Look to anyone you can think of that has led a remarkable life – each of those people at some point in their lives said 'enough' to following a well-worn route and instead chose to step out of the confines and into the unknown. Each one of them looked ahead by setting in motion the intent to do something greater instead. What takes a remarkable life into the realms of greatness is when our life is in service to something greater than the self.

Daring to be great is to connect with a sense of the self in relation to the universe. It's a recognition that there is something beyond the self. For some it is religious in nature, for some it is an unknown quality – difficult to name but nonetheless there. A quality that speaks of the sacredness of life itself – that is life-affirming, not life-destroying. A quality that is boundless and free. It is a quality that is everywhere, yet it cannot be seen. It surrounds us, yet we cannot physically touch it. What we can do is open up our hearts to whatever it is we know can only take us to a far better place.

I believe in something that is bigger than humans but which I find difficult to define. This for me is also a quest for peace. I know deep in my heart it can be done, and I believe we can, in daring to be great, reach out and create a world of peace. It matters not whether you are a Buddhist or an atheist, a humanist or a spiritualist. A deeper wisdom applies to us all: a wisdom that starts from a premise of 'first do no harm'. I invite you all – whether spiritually engaged or not – to join me in this quest. For me, my quest embodies all that I am doing to end the era of ecocide.

So, here is my commitment: I dare to be great in my lifetime and I dare to share what I learn with you. It may be a journey that is fraught with difficulties, but my commitment is to continue, no matter what. By sharing what I experience I hope to inspire you to do the same; it is also a way of passing on a legacy to the future. I choose to do this in the public realm, so that I can speak publicly about what I learn and I say this: I embrace a world of abundance and love. I am fearless (sometimes) and am at peace (most of the time). I am empowering the flow of funding into a world where the wellbeing of people and planet come first.

It's a challenge I have set myself – not just in my public speaking, but in the small moments of my life when I am given a chance to step up or walk away. I dare to be great. I have discovered that something happens when we set an intent. Life throws us opportunities to meet the challenge. Our world takes on a different hue. Suddenly life becomes an adventure. My work advocating a law that puts the health and wellbeing of people and planet first is no longer a job, but a quest. I do not know what will come next, but I trust that each step will lead to another that will help me on my way.

I do not have a job-spec. When we direct ourselves and take charge of our lives (set our moral compass to great), we create a space for something new to emerge. Greatness lies within each of us, it's there – it is our choice whether or not we access it. Like a kernel that has been in hibernation, it is there ready to grow as soon as it is watered. Withhold the water at the early stages and it may die, but the more we can feed and give nourishment as the seed germinates, the more likely it is to thrive. Just as when a seed turns into a plant, when we are called upon to be great something akin to magic happens.

What I am discovering in my quest is that to access greatness I must step out of my comfort zone and face my dark side. I have had to enter my inner world of unresolved conflict. Sometimes I really did not want to look, but when

I did, I discovered that I was able to let go of much that had been holding me back. These are moments of great release, the moments when we face a cycle of harm playing out in our own lives and say, 'enough, no more'. There is huge power in that phrase: it's more than choice, it's a point of clarity where we decide to take a different path.

What is your commitment? Please do take your time to fine-tune your answer. And, when you hear that answer – does it make your heart sing?

That's a sure indicator that you are on the right path. If you think, 'I want to be great so that I make lots of money', go further again. This is not the kind of greatness I am talking about. I speak of aligning our values to something greater than the self, not simply making money for money's sake. If it's finance that drives you, and you find yourself sitting back waiting for funds to arrive before you follow your quest, then you are not opening yourself up to greatness.

Money, or the lack of it, need not hinder a life of greatness – if anything it can enhance it. Gifts in kind come from many directions; creativity is then unfettered by cost-analysis and as a result different routes can be taken. The opportunity here is to be the greatest we can be, in service to something greater than the self, not to get an income. It is not always easy – but that is part of the adventure. After all, if it was that easy, we'd all be doing it already!

Vision of Greatness Key

What does greatness look like to you? Free your mind to conjure up an image; it may be faintly ridiculous or it may be childlike, but that's all to the better. Go with it – an odd image has so much more power to return and stay with us than something that looks like a glossy magazine cover. Our power to envision greatness helps anchor our intent. Once you have your image of greatness, allow it to surface as and when you feel you have a challenge to meet. By doing that, each time your image appears in your mind's eye, you are connecting to that part of your being that says, 'I am great and I can meet this'.

From Being to Doing

I have found that practising greatness takes some doing. It feels good, but it's all too easy to sit back and leave it for another day. It's like choosing to get fit or to eat more healthily – it takes self-will. It's the same as when I choose to adopt practices that enhance my greatness. Some days, it has to be said, I fall off the wagon. No matter, it's not the falling that counts, it's the learning that comes each time I meet a stumbling block.

Greatness, it seems, lies within even the most seemingly unpromising situation; in fact sometimes that is where it can rise up even faster. Those moments of turnaround, which even the most hard-hearted can experience, the breaking of a cycle of harm, the volte-face that no one expects – they can and do happen. A window opens and that is the moment when greatness can blow in. It may be unnoticed by others, but it matters not – what matters is whether we are open to receiving the change. And when we do open ourselves up by embracing that moment, imperceptible as that may be to anyone else, we are contributing to something greater. What difference, you may ask, does it make to have one person on a quest of greatness? Each one of us is like a drop in the ocean. But each drop of greatness is like a homeopathic drop – adding to the rising tide of harmony as it readies to wash in. Precisely how many drops are required is unknown. However, drop by drop, every moment of greatness contributes first to a ripple, then to a wave, then it becomes so big a new surge forms, coming so fast and strong that no longer is it difficult to fight against the tide – the tide itself turns and we find ourselves in the flow.

Like the tide washing in, we are bringing into being a new process – playing at how to be great. As with all new games, at first it may seem as if you are missing the mark, but that's not true. Stick with it, play with it and make the space for yourself to check in. Like a stone that shines when it's polished, so too does greatness. Through continued use of your newly found way of being, your rough-cut stone turns into a gem. You'll find your responses quickening and soon enough you increasingly know instinctively what and how to respond. And when you miss the opportunity to shine, no worries, life has a great way of affording us the chance to shine time and again.

In my immediate world, I notice that the more thought I give to something, the clearer I become. Clarity is key to conscious creation. I *choose* to put my energies into my vision of a better world for the whole of the wider Earth community. Earth is a living being – she gives us life and we have a reciprocal role – to give life back. In so doing, I feel energised and feel the pull of a world free from conflict, a world with greater freedom for all. It is my vision of something greater that has led me to face the ecocides I see. I cannot ignore them, but have 0to face them squarely – for me as a lawyer it has been a journey of exploration, giving definition to and finding out how we can bring significant harm to an end. Ecocide is extensive damage, destruction to or loss of ecosystems – and it makes no sense to commit ecocide. Ultimately, we all suffer – all human and non-human beings. Ecocide is both a personal and a collective harm. Yet, the greatness lies in each of us to take up the mantle and become voices for the Earth.

It may well be that once you open yourself to daring to be great, life brings you experiences you would never have considered before or that you thought were wacky, without sound scientific backing or just plain bizarre. Remain open and you may find that a different perspective on life greatly enhances your vision. We can never know what lies ahead if we remain contained inside our box. The gift is the offering of a new pathway – and it's ours to explore, whether it be a new way of learning more about ourselves or stepping out of our comfort zones. Because it's only when we take the leap that we allow ourselves to receive the bounty of the gift. Park your preconceived judgements, let the new flow in and discern if it works for you or not – for some it's simply a matter of exploring the forbidden, for others it's an opportunity to review what has been closed before now. Whatever it is you choose to explore, know that your innate is there to guide you.

There is great power that can be harnessed through the pursuit of greatness. I talk here of the power to effect greatness within our lives that contributes to a better world, a world where we no longer cause ecocide; a world where all forms of harm are significantly abated – cultural, ecological and self-harm. Such power brings with it the responsibility to use, not abuse, it for the greatest purpose. By taking responsibility for our most powerful state of being, we cultivate the most powerful state of doing. What is the greatness within you? It's there – and it'll keep on coming back to you now, as if tugging at your sleeve to say, 'What say you? This has to be addressed.' Look around: is anyone else looking through the same lens, attempting to answer the same question? No one has ownership of a good idea, so let's share it. Give up the territorial claim – big questions call on more than just one person to bring about the answer. It may well be that others are already working in the same space and a broader approach may help; so let's build alliances, reach out to others and be inclusive – bring in unlikely allies. Wherever we intersect, these are the synapse connection points and the potential to interconnect. Blur the boundaries and look to the margins – that's where the most fertile ground is, not in the centre of the establishment. Invite in other voices: male, female, indigenous, religious.Open up the narrative. Sometimes asking big questions calls on our courage to stand up and speak out, even when to do so brings us face to face with authorities. Explore the question 'what is' and take a stand on what you believe in – even if no one is seemingly with you. To challenge those in authority is to call into question those who have made decisions on our behalf – and this is valid, in particular when decisions are being made that may lead to significant harm. Take it further if need be, non-compliance takes courage as well; civil disobedience is the daring to stand up and speak out from the heart. Refuse to be boxed in, in fact throw away the box. Free yourself to speak truth to power – ask the questions, challenge the norm and voice your concerns. Only by doing this can we discover the answers, answers that lead us to a world where we are free – free from harm.

You are on a quest – and to be on a quest is to seek, to ask, to challenge. You are the seeker of a greater truth. To be on a quest is to ask questions as you go, questions of the self and the non-self, and to find out how to reach the answers. Many new lands shall be crossed before the quest is over and many challenges met along the way – there will be crossroads, blind alleys and beautiful vistas on the horizon. Each person you meet is there to help in some way, sometimes known, sometimes not. Open your heart and open your mind, take the leap and you will find great answers beyond your wildest dreams.

Open Question Key

Asking a question which you do not know the answer to opens up a wider spectrum. Open questions are not the kind of question that can be given a textbook answer – they're questions that lead to a deeper kind of enquiry. Have you ever had a moment when you asked, 'What next?' or when you framed a question that began with 'How on earth do I?' These are the sort of open questions that penetrate the soul and call on us to look inwards to examine how to sincerely respond. Invite them in. These sorts of questions are innate: open questions that open up the space. It's a different kind of compass that can help here; our inner compass guiding us all the way. It takes a new kind of approach – one that we are not taught at school. The answer may not be immediate or what we expect, but that is the beauty of an innate response, it comes from the heart instead of the head. It feels good, it feels right and it feels for the best. The more we ask innate open questions, the more we tap into the space where our own innate wisdom comes into play without agenda or ego. Sometimes the answers we receive come through others, and sometimes we hear them within our own thoughts – where they come from is not so important, it's the ability to listen and to respond when we hear the answer that matters.

My Story: Ugly Duckling

A few years back I took a walk past my old school – it was the first time I had felt able and willing to go and look at it, such was the pain I felt about my time there. For me, this was a way of letting go. I had been bullied and badly hurt by my experience there and I no longer wanted it to haunt me. I remember feeling very lonely, mocked for being fat and for wearing glasses.

I had no friends and I was picked on by one girl relentlessly. Lunchtime and breaks were a form of torture, feeling unwanted wherever I went. I did not know how to reach out and ask for help. I could not see a path that would take me out of this hell. The school system was a relic of Victorian times – speaking about feelings and showing emotion was not approved of.

In my mind's eye I could see myself back then, so afraid of life and everyone around me. I feel a huge surge of sadness for the child I was. I can see now how deeply unhappy a time it was and how much I internalised the pain. I had learned not to be visible; I held back, I kept quiet and I retreated into myself. I did not know how to cope so I shut down. Every step I took up the hill to the school brought back the sense of being rejected.

I stood in wonder at what I saw; here was a school boarded up and left to decay. It was as if it had never existed. The very bricks and mortar of the place were crumbling. What seemed so set in stone in my own head was here in front of me falling apart.

And in that moment, I realised: maybe I too can let go. I turn away and feel as if I am shedding a huge weight. Enough, I say to myself, I choose to live life another way.

FIRST STEPS

Being Open to the Call

He was standing near the edge. A fast train was approaching a busy station and the elderly man next to him slipped and fell onto the track. Holding two children by the hand, our man turned to the person beside him to safeguard his kids, and he jumped. He grabbed the fallen man, pulled him in-between the rail tracks and threw himself on top of his body. That second, the train ran right over without touching either of them. Both survived.

Asked later why he did it, our man said, 'Something had to be done.' He knew he had to act. He spoke in the language of necessity. He had no choice, even though he had two children in his care. What precisely made him take action when there were others also standing there on the platform who could have acted? He heard the call.

The elderly man who fell may have shouted if he could, but it didn't require him to make a sound; his plight was heard at a higher level by our man on the platform – and he responded. What happened next was a moment of greatness. For some reason, the young man who leapt to save the old man's life had no thought of fear. Had he paused for one moment, it would have been too late; but he seemingly had no thoughts of 'What should I do if I get it wrong?' or 'But I can't because I have to keep the children safe'. In fact, he trusted a stranger beside him to look after his children, jumped without knowing what he'd do and acted from a place of instinct. It took incredible courage to do that – he acted from the heart to prevent an unknown man's death.

Sometimes these moments are fleeting; the call comes and the moment to act is there and then. No time to stop to work it out – it is simply a moment of crystal-clear innate knowingness that speaks of something far greater than the self. The drive is so strong that nothing in the world can stop the power to act at that point in time. It is an act of the divine.

There are many stories like this one – when the unremarkable becomes remarkable. Some are better known than others. Take Sophie Scholl. Now one of Germany's national treasures, outside her own country she is hardly known at all. Sophie Scholl, a Munich University student, was executed for revealing the truth about the activities of the Nazi authorities. Sophie Scholl and the White Rose movement she inspired stood up and took direct non-violent action. Their crime was the dissemination of leaflets highlighting and decrying the tyranny of the Nazi dictatorship. It was a decision to undertake something unlawful – an act of civil disobedience that they believed was a necessity – to halt a greater but unnamed crime, a crime that cost many lives. That crime did not have a name at that time. But it soon did: genocide.

Sophie and her friends were unsupported by the law back then; they were the criminals in the eyes of the court for daring to speak out. Sophie and her co-conspirators were denied the right to defend themselves in their trial. They were convicted for resorting to unlawful acts, which they believed to be necessary to speak the truth. To make a law sometimes you have to break a law – and Sophie knew this. At the very end of her trial, Sophie spoke out. It is just a matter of time, she said, before the true destroyers are put in the dock. Sophie and her fellow accused were all executed for speaking out. Records show that Sophie and her brother Hans knew the risks of getting caught; they had discussed that they, and possibly their parents, could lose their lives, yet they still spoke out. Why did they do this? They heard the call.

Back then, the tyranny was Nazism. Today, it is pursuit of profit without moral compass or responsibility. Back then the crime was genocide. Today the crime is ecocide. Resetting the collective moral compass today is proving an even greater challenge, but it is resetting. More and more people are hearing the call – a call that is coming directly from the Earth – and taking action in nations across the world. More and more people are discovering their ability to respond. For some, it is a matter of life or death. Such action takes greatness and every time we each take action, speak out and shine a light on where there is harm, we reset our own inner compass and pave the way for others coming behind us.

My Story: Choice Point

I sat in the Court of Appeal in the Royal Courts of Justice waiting for judgement. I was in a courtroom at the top of the building, looking out over rooftops and trees below. It was judgement day. I let my mind wander out of the window and up into the sky. I found myself thinking, 'It's not just my client that has been badly harmed and injured, so has the Earth.' I could see in my mind's eye vast tracts of land destroyed, trees decimated, rivers poisoned, skies filled with pollution. 'Something has to be done about this.' The next thought changed my life. I thought, 'The Earth's in need of a good lawyer.'

Stepping Into the Unknown

That was my choice point; I heard the call. I didn't know it then, but I do now – the quest had begun. I couldn't get it out of my head – what if I was to represent the Earth in court? Could I speak on her behalf? After all, I could speak on behalf of fictional legal persons, such as companies, so why not the Earth? But there was missing law. My big question that followed was: how do we create a legal duty of care for the Earth?

Choice points are the crossroads in our lives – do we choose to continue on the same path or do we choose to step onto an unknown route? It's the junction in the middle of the road – only we can decide which way to go. I didn't know it then, but

I had decided to step off my path of being a well-paid barrister and choose a route that was completely unknown to me. Had I known beforehand what was to come, I probably would have said 'no way!', but now that I have, I am so grateful for the challenges. Those nagging thoughts of 'is this all there is to life?' – making large sums of money from fighting cases in court – wouldn't go away. I was spending increasingly more time trying to make sense of all the growing injustice I was seeing around me, especially the horrors being inflicted upon the Earth by big transnational companies who could not be stopped by law. My vision was of a world where restorative justice prevailed, not the huge corruption I was seeing playing out. This corruption simply did not correlate with my sense that the world is driven by love, not war. What I was seeing did not make me happy. Something had to be done.

Choice Point Key

Choice points occur more often than we realise; sometimes in small ways, but even the small ones are like ripples on a sea, enough of them and a sea-change occurs. Globally, we have come to a choice point – do we stay with business as usual or do we take another route? How you choose to engage with the world has impact. Often we are unaware of the consequences of our actions, but sometimes when we take a moment to let our mind wander up and out the window we can gain a different perspective on the world. Like a glider catching a thermal, we can soar above the world and look down and easily see what it is that does not work.

If we can see the bigger picture, and if it's an image that does not work, we can always find a way to change the outcome. All it takes is a vision of something far better.

My Story: The Quest Begins

The quest began the moment I stepped out of court – I looked around: who else was out there creating new laws for the Earth? Something new, I felt, was ready to emerge. It was as if the question, 'How do we create a legal duty of care for the Earth?' was pulling me forward. If we do not care for the Earth, I thought, then we shall end up in a world where only those who fight for their lives survive. That was not my vision – and it was not one I was prepared to see play out.

Inviting in the Emergency

There's a natural governance when an ecosystem is functioning at its best: for something new to emerge, sometimes a certain amount of clearing has to occur first. A forest fire can clear the way for something new to grow – it may look like all has been destroyed, but in fact that which has been burned provides food for the new shoots. The old is sacrificed for the new, and regeneration begins once again. To the untrained human eye it can look like an emergency when we see a forest burning, whereas it may well be part of a larger lifecycle. It may seem to be an extreme way of balancing nature but if the system is so out of kilter, then nature has a habit of restoring harmony, sometimes through very dramatic means.

We are in truth part of nature ourselves; our own ecosystem is sometimes so out of kilter that the moment of emergency arrives. A tipping point can take many forms, the most extreme being collapse. We fear emergencies – yet an emergency is, after all, just a state of emergence, a point in time when something new can emerge.

Globally our Earth's ecosystem is rapidly tipping out of kilter. What do we do? Sit back and let nature run its course? I cannot square it with my conscience to be complicit in something that's a ticking time bomb for future generations; I know that much of our human activity has caused this sorry state of affairs and I know that we can reset our compass and rectify the imbalance. But something is missing here, something that unites us all. How can we stop significant harm from occurring not just here and now, but for all future time? It's not enough to halt an ecocide over here to then have it occurring over there. Everywhere I look there is mass damage and destruction playing out every day – and it's not a crime. Some governments have suspended or removed key environmental protection laws at a national level so that profits can be accrued; businesses lobby for new laws to give them more powers, at the expense of the health and wellbeing of people and planet, there are even tax breaks for those who comply and bribes to turn a blind eye. Law has made it all possible. Not all law works and just now the scales of justice are out of kilter.

Law, it seems, is no longer about justice. But it should be. We have ended up with laws that have increasingly tied us up in knots. So, let's declare an emergency; let's decouple the systems that no longer work by making them illegal, creating greater freedom for the emergence of something better, something premised on a 'first do no harm' principle.

Natural Law Key

We are also governed by laws that are called natural laws. Natural laws are laws that, despite not being written down on paper and imposed through a legal system as we know it, are applied to our lives whether or not we are aware of it. Martin Luther King Jr believed that there are two types of laws in this world: those that are made by a higher authority and those that are made by humans. And not until all the laws that are made by humans are consistent with the laws that are made by the higher authority will we live in a just world.

Ask yourself one powerful question of any law or decision: whose interests are being protected here? If the answer is the polluter rather than people and planet, you'll know that the law is misaligned. Natural law is aligned with the sanctity of life, not the killing of life.

HELP ARRIVES

 *My Story: The Lightbulb Moment*

Just before I left for the Copenhagen climate negotiations, a good friend gave me some wisdom: 'Only when we face the shadow self and give it name can the healing begin.' Sometimes a phrase or a sentence boomerangs around inside our heads – what did this mean? It's as if all that mass damage and destruction out there was our collective shadow, but it didn't have a name. It was a phrase that stayed with me. Was there someone out there who could give me the word I was seeking?

Seated on a platform with a British journalist called George Monbiot, I found my answer. Someone in the audience said, 'We need a new language to deal with this mass damage and destruction.' A lightbulb went off in my head – 'This guy's right, it's like genocide – only it's ecocide. That should be a crime.'

It was like a lightning bolt – here was what was missing: a Law of Ecocide, based on the no-harm concept.

Three months later in 2010, I proposed to the United Nations a written submission for an international Law of Ecocide, not only to put in place a prohibition on significant harm but also to create a legal duty of care. By creating such a law at an international level, in one fell swoop our national laws could no longer put profit first. Instead, by creating a Law of Ecocide, mass damage and destruction would be outlawed and an overriding duty of care for people and planet would take precedence. And to do this only requires an amendment to the Rome Statute (the treaty that established the International Criminal Court).

Flipping the Norm

It took me quite some time to unravel the threads of law. Taking each one back to its source, researching some of the world's leading authorities and texts led me to a deeper insight and clarity of understanding of what law was, is and could be. More than that, I was seeking a fast-track route, something that would turn everything around on a pin – something that would flip the norm. Could there be a way?

Much later I discovered that the word already existed. Even more, a Law of Ecocide very nearly became an international crime back in the 1990s but at the eleventh hour it was removed from the draft text of the Rome Statute.[1] So here it was, a missing crime that had been shelved. Thanks to pivotal research undertaken by Dr Damian Short and some of his students at the University of London, we now have a paper trail of its removal at a closed-door meeting in 1996 with no reason given.[2]

Two books I have written set out the draft Ecocide Law,[3] and every nation has been sent a Concept Paper[4] that sets out a pathway to include Ecocide Law in the Rome Statute. What I have subsequently come to realise is that politics (on the whole – but there are exceptions) has become numbed-out from taking the steps to bring to an end a world where mass damage and destruction drive our businesses at the very highest levels. Something has caused our leaders to fear taking the quantum leap to break the cycle of harm that is costing humanity so much more than money. This has much to do with the entrenched belief in the value of money over and above the welfare of our wider Earth community; a belief that has become a norm because of law. It is the law to put the interests of the shareholders first, which means to put profit first.

So here we have a moment in time where we collectively have a choice point – do we continue with business and politics as usual or do we radically turn around and take a very different path forward? A Law of Ecocide provides a very clear break with a system that no longer works. It disrupts the prevailing norm. No longer can we put profit first. An International Crime has huge power as it acts as umbrella law; no nation can override it. The power of a Law of Ecocide is nothing less than great. It has the power to seed something that will have a dramatically profound effect on all of our lives and on all who come after us – to vastly reduce the harm, pain and suffering that affects all of the wider Earth community.

Sometimes a law comes along that has the potential to change our frame of reference altogether – a touchstone that serves as a reminder of what it is we most value: harm or harmony, war or peace, profit or people and planet; the scarcity of life or the sacredness of life; lack or love. The former feeds an uncontrollable sense of fear, the latter is born of a sense of a duty of care.

The First Nations of Canada and America have their own narrative and stories, one of which speaks powerfully about a story based on fear, control, greed and ecocide. The Wendigo is a mythological creature with an insatiable appetite. The Wendigo represents a culture that is self-destructing by destroying all it touches in pursuit of feeding a demand for more and more. But the more it destroys in its wake, the more the harm escalates to enormous proportions – to such an extent that the Wendigo is left with nothing else save himself, and so he self-destructs. To break the cycle of harm before the inevitable collapse seems to be an impossible task, yet it can be done. The Wendigo loses its power as soon as we give name to the harm – ecocide. Because, by naming it, the cycle is disrupted.

Breaking patterns of harm requires a disruptor. By naming the harm, the power it exerted as an unknown entity is gone. The crucial first step is taken to derail the train of destruction. But, wait a minute – what is happening here? We are repeating the same patterns of harm, time and time again. What if we flipped this and set in place something new; new patterns, that are based on a different set of values, which when repeated serve to reinforce a completely new normative. New patterns building cumulatively upon each other and with each other to create a whole new story of the world – a new story that more accurately reflects the emergent values of our time. Indeed, what is required is nothing less than a completely new story of our time. Where to start? New stories never begin in the heart of establishment – they start in the margins then grow and grow. Ecocide Law is part of the new story that is emerging.

It's a challenging thought, putting people and planet before profit. That flips our norm. But that's not to say we lose out. If anything, we all stand to gain by the flow of thought, action and money being directed by our values.

When we value the health and wellbeing of humanity and all beings first and foremost, we replace an imposed value – ecosystem services – with intrinsic value. Sacredness of life takes precedence and our duty becomes a sacred duty of care. Conscious intent of where our money flows – into non-harmful activity – realigns our values with our finance. Money, after all, is just a physical form of intent. So, where do we choose our money to flow to? Put our money into the hands of a few who invest in dangerous industrial activities and it literally becomes toxic; let it flow into that which affirms life for all, and our contribution effects a great change. In so doing, the Law of Ecocide creates a legal duty of care for our global commons. Our global economy no longer operates from the profit imperative. This is actually a return to the original meaning of the word 'economy' – stewardship of our home.[5]

Ecocide Law changes the flow of money. No longer will it be possible to invest in unlawful activities, nor will it be lawful to put in place policy or finance that drives the wheels of an ecocidal global economy. Ecocide puts the definitive spoke in the wheel – it disrupts the cart before it careers off the cliff.

Ecocide Law, you may say, is a great idea. Ideas, however, are only great if they are given life. To give a Law of Ecocide life requires sign-off by two-thirds of member states of the International Criminal Court. Right now that means eighty-two nations of the world. Or rather, eighty-two leaders: eighty-two leaders who could do something truly great on behalf of the people of their nations. Our leaders need to stand up and dare to be great. Well, maybe it's up to us, who are calling on our leaders, who speak on our behalf, to dare to be great too. After all, how can we ask someone to do something we have not yet learned to do ourselves?

A Different Kind of Conversation

A different kind of conversation is emerging and taking root; one based on speaking from the heart. I hear it more and more everywhere I go. Speaking to something greater than the self invites in a conversation of a very different kind. Firstly, it's a conversation, not a monologue; an exchange based on free will and friendship. Secondly, what makes it different from conversations we have normally is that it is an explicit seeking out of a complete boundless repository of out-of-the-box big ideas and super-good advice. A repository that can be tapped into at will and put to best use. In other words – the very best source there is. Thirdly, it's about care.

So, when we speak to something greater than the self, all that emanates from there can only be for the greater purpose. What that greater purpose is, is different for each of us. For me, the greater purpose is to encourage and bring into being new pathways where peace, not war, prevail. A place of greater freedom for all. It was a deeper enquiry that opened up this vision for me, but this was only possible when I understood that I could be here for a greater reason than simply to survive. We are here to thrive. One day I really got it – we are ultimately all one. I had a moment when I lay on the Earth and I felt it. And I knew what I felt was premised on a sense of my deep interconnectedness. But it is more than that: I actually feel deep love for this Earth.

My Story: Plugging into the Bigger Picture

I'm lying on a grassy hillside and I feel as if I've become part of the Earth; my breath has slowed down as if I'm about to fall asleep, but then something happens that I can hardly explain.

I feel energy surging through me, from my toes right up to the top of my head. It's delicious. I have a heightened sense of my surroundings.

I got Gaia'd. It's as if I am plugged into the Earth's energy system. And being plugged into a greater whole makes my synapses tingle. I'm like a light that has been switched on – and I feel very much alive because of it. I'm on-grid, but this is a super grid that connects all beings across the world. This is one mega-electric network of free and boundless energy that flows between us all. As the energy flows more and more, so too does my growing sense of a far bigger picture.

Plugging-in Key

How often do you slip off your shoes and connect to the Earth? Rubber, concrete and asphalt all sever our direct connection to our energetic field of wellbeing. Find a park, a patch of grass, or a tree to connect with. Feel the energy tingling from your toes up, and visualise Earth energy as a light surging through you into every atom, every cell of your being. It may take practice to feel it, but with time you will connect as soon as you turn your thoughts to the Earth.

What I feel, science is now exploring.[6] We now know that the Earth has its own state of being; if you are to take a reading from the Earth you will discover that it resonates at 7.8 hertz. This equates to Theta wave activity, often experienced when we drift off to sleep or are in an advanced state of hypnosis or meditation. Whenever we choose, we can slow down our brainwaves to a Theta state. The benefit of this is that it opens up the space where intent can be set.

By slowing down our own brainwave activity to align with the Earth's frequency ('getting Gaia'd'), we allow ourselves to experience a dream-like state whilst awake. When I first discovered this simple fact, I felt a sense of wonderment; 7.8 Hz is something we all can – and do – step into when we are fully present. Children can play for hours in a Theta state, fully absorbed, present and content. When we are in a Theta space, our capacity to expand our abilities is exponentially increased – this is why children find it so easy to absorb new languages, expressions and be creative. We can too. Each of us can return to that state. It's there, albeit like a rusty cog, a bit of practice is required before our internal wheels start turning again.

Sacred Space

Theta, in non-technical terms, is the slowing down of our brainwave activity enough to allow space for something new to emerge (be it language, visions, ideas, insight). It's a sacred space, a place to explore and create, and a place to face, let go or release beliefs that hold us back.

Sacred Space Key

We look to grow so many other things in life yet when it comes to self-growth, there never seems to be the time. Too much to do, too busy. Please pause here – does this ring true for you? If it does, set the intent to remedy it. It can be transformational. Give yourself sacred space, even if it's just for a few minutes first thing in the morning when you waken. No need to get out of bed, just take a moment to connect to Earth and check-in with your innate.

My practice of entering into my sacred space is a form of Askesis. For me, Askesis is a political act, an act of spiritual governance. How we choose to govern our lives and, consequently, how we choose to invite in and participate with outer governance systems, such as local and global politics, can be explored through Askesis and the application of aligning our inner self-determination with our outer world. Our values that we choose to shape our inner state of being become increasingly reflected in our outer state of doing. When there is a connection between our being and doing, it becomes easier to decide what is for the best in the greater scheme of things. No longer do we perceive ourselves as separate entities; the self has become part of a far greater entity.

Askesis denotes any kind of practical training or exercise. Harking back to the ancient Greeks, it was commonplace to learn any kind of art or technique by Mathesis and Askesis – by theoretical knowledge and practical training. The Askesis of the Greeks had a very specific purpose: the establishment of a relationship of self-possession and self-sovereignty to prepare for, and have set in place the 'moral equipment that will permit [a person] to fully confront the world in an ethical and rational manner'.[7] This was to experience the practice of philosophy as a way of becoming who one is: the work of self-formation.

Through my practice of Askesis, I have consciously decided to explore my state of being in concert with the Earth. Askesis takes mindfulness to another level, to the next stage on from self-awareness and moment-by-moment intentionality, to a place where I can direct and set in place new patterns. By consciously embracing my own self-autonomy and self-responsibility, I recalibrate, aligning with a greater energy field where I can access a greater state of being. By practising on a daily basis, my line of connection between myself and the 'something greater than the self' strengthens every day. Also known as a 'technology of the self', Askesis can liberate us from what Michel Foucault, the French philosopher, called 'previous cultural circuits'. Foucault observed what he called the possibility to create new 'privileged spaces'. Stepping into a privileged or sacred space, gives us the opportunity to break the old patterns of harm, so that we can finally let them go.

Tuning Key

You know the moments, points in time when we react badly or we get hooked in to something harmful. Well, these are gold-dust moments. Catch them and you become an alchemist. Take a harm and transform it into harmony. Like a record caught in the same groove, you can stop it. Lift the stylus, flip the record and play a new tune.

This is how to disrupt your own pattern. Name it and let it go. One of the easiest ways to do that is to say simply: 'Enough, no more.' Give it vision – write it down and burn it as you say it. The hardest bit is to name the pattern – but once you have done that, the rest is easy.

Self-formation creates the most powerful force within; we create what Foucault called our own 'biopower', where we are in charge of our state of being. Once we begin to be nourished from a source that we determine, the empty self recedes. By creating our own biopower, we find ourselves stepping back and discerning how we choose to live. For every person who chooses to speak out on their own terms, hundreds more are empowered to do the same.

On a collective level, cooperation with decentralised, self-determining community governance takes precedence. Askesis is the practice of taking back governance and choosing self-care. Expanding self-care to Earth-care opens up yet more questions; systems that are seemly fixed in stone begin to crumble. How we choose to engage with health, business and politics shifts: no longer do we accept without question decisions made by others that do not accord with our own state of being. Instead we literally reclaim our own power.

By being nourished at a deeper level, our capacity for care expands and it no longer shapes just our state of being – our state of doing naturally aligns itself, and where there is a disconnect it becomes untenable to ignore it. The capacity to care is also an activity: something to be cultivated, protected and improved. Moving from self-care to Earth-care is an expansion of the self into the realm of greatness.

By expanding our cycle of harmony to include all beings, we contribute to the bigger picture. But take note: first comes the care of the self – if there is no mastery of care for the self, how do we learn how to forge the necessary connections to care for the wider Earth community?

INNER JOURNEY

Quests inevitably lead the questor to take a parallel journey into the inner world, which cannot be ignored. If anything, to ignore it is to abandon the quest. For it is within our deepest exploration of the self that we gain our most profound insight.

Greatness comes with a very big dose of inner-sight capacity and the ability to meet even the most hidden parts of our being. Understanding what makes ourselves tick and seeing the direct correlation between our being and doing (and how we can resolve our own conflicts) gives us far greater guidance as to how we can resolve the seemingly unresolvable elsewhere. Likewise, sometimes the inner-sight comes by viewing things from the opposite end of the spectrum and looking to the collective pattern at play to find the key to unlock it.

From Conflict to Catalyst

Acceptance of self-harm (which includes our buy-in to cultural assumptions that harm is sometimes necessary) is an open-door policy for inviting conflict. So how do we resolve collective conflict – such as the acceptance of harming our Earth?

Conflict – to fight – brings with it trauma. For the person who has suffered, often their perception of the trauma is passive (in the sense that they did not choose to experience the pain); life has thrown a knock-out event that brings with it harm, suffering and loss. Pain can be revisited time and again, or it can be released.

So how does the decision to no longer engage with conflict play out on a collective level? Firstly, it takes a seeking out; a calling for another way of resolving the conflict to emerge – an openness, if you like, to seeing that there is another route.

And indeed this is the case; here we are at a crossroads and two signs emerge to point in different directions – one points to catalyst, the other to conflict. When we perceive conflict as something we choose to engage in (or not) we can then make informed decisions as to how we respond. When we take the path of conflict, we are quite literally chained and locked-in. We cannot see that we can choose to let go. We cannot see that we can choose to say, 'stop; enough, no more.' (Have you ever reached the point with something that it becomes so unbearable that you say, 'I've had it; I'm not taking any more of this abuse'?) When that happens, the chains are broken. Collectively, when a group of individuals say, 'enough, no more' there is a space, a moment in time to choose a different path. That path can lead to a greater freedom. All it takes is a surprisingly few people choosing a different path for something new to emerge. Apply that to ecocide and what can occur collectively is a breaking of a cycle of harm that keeps on playing out every day. And by creating that space for something new to emerge the call is heard by new players who can bring forward a different mindset.

What does this say about our political world? Could it be that when we begin to say, 'Enough, this must end' to the decisions of our political system, that the tides around us change direction? I believe so. Each ripple we send out is felt by others who then contribute to the mounting wave of intent – either politics as we know it shifts with us or it collapses. When a vision of something new emerges into new space, new players step forward. This is another choice point: to fight against the new tide, or to choose to go with the flow. It could be a moment to step aside and allow others to steer. If it truly is a moment of choice, then that person is shifting their own perception which in turn allows them to move forward, because they are no longer stuck in conflict. For many, however, the fight simply continues and the cycle of harm plays out yet again. Conflict can play out in many ways, it may be public or private – either way, a political leader may be deposed, step down, be removed or voted out. The same happens in business. Yet, although the cycle of harm may appear to be broken, if the system does not change (and that applies equally to our own internal system as well as to the external system that we engage in), the cycle of harm will reappear soon enough and play out again and again until it is finally disrupted.

When we let go of our own inner conflict, we open up the space – the opportunity to be a catalyst for greater good is suddenly there. A very powerful example of a great man who stepped out from being imprisoned by both physical and mental means, and who became the catalyst for enormous change, had this to say: 'As I walked out the door toward my freedom, I knew that if I did not leave all the anger, hatred and bitterness behind that I would still be in prison.' Nelson Mandela understood what it was to be free.

Nelson Mandela worked with collective conflict resolution – he and many unnamed others who effected great change, freeing up the path for many blacks and whites to come together, marry, share their lives, hopes and dreams – and he understood it well. But he knew he had to let go of his own personal conflict before he could step up to something bigger than his self. He recognised that great change only comes about through the greatness of humanity. Greatness, he understood, is a collective endeavour that starts from the personal and is something to aspire to individually and together. 'Sometimes,' Mandela said, 'it falls upon a generation to be great. You can be that great generation. Let your greatness blossom.' Each time collective conflict arises, it is an opportunity for each of us to decide whether to choose to react or respond. When we react, we are tapping into an earlier source of pain. Numbing-out is a form of reacting, albeit passively. Thus conflict can play out in society time and again, especially when there is no insight that any other route can be taken. History repeats itself until more and more people choose to break the cycle of harm and take charge of their own lives. One form of breaking the cycle of harm is when a community sets forth its own commitment to adhere to a different set of norms or values. Another form is when enough people stop fighting and instead speak out for a greater freedom from a place of deep care. The protestor becomes a protector. This calls on deep reserves within us to let go of the conflict we feel, yet speak out and call for an end to the harm being caused. Only when that happens are we no longer enslaved by the conflict and often at that point we become catalysts for others to do the same.

Is it possible to love and at the same time respond to conflict? I believe so. This is not to sidestep or wash over a source of harm; on the contrary, it is the ultimate match. To stand up to conflict from a place of love is to go to the source without bitterness or hatred. It is a moment of facing the shadow. When we face the shadow with love and speak from the heart, something shifts. If we know that the conflict represents a deeper harm that has yet to be healed, then the power of intent to bring it to an end touches us deeply. The more we meet conflict with words and actions of peace, consciously and with love, the greater the strength of resolve. There comes a point where something has to give, and harm gives way to harmony.

Anger can serve to fuel us, constructively or destructively. Harness its energy with love and we have the power to change the world. That is when we become catalysts – we literally shift energy within. Instead of anger turning into something toxic inside of us, we meet it with love and ride the wave. So let it ride, let it flow – into something far greater. Let it be the fuel that powers our own rocket, and let's head for the stars.

Responding from a place of deep care opens up the space to meet conflict and say, 'I see you and I do not accept your harm.' Identifying the conflict as a harm and giving it a name is hugely empowering. Bearing witness and giving a name brings to the surface that which is required to be remedied.

Purging the Pain

Often, we are taught that to show emotion is a weakness – a symptom of something flawed within, an instability or something that speaks of a failure to stand strong. Typically, we push it down, tell ourselves to let it go and yet it has a habit of surging up. And when it does, sometimes the fallout lands on others around us. Purging the pain means taking the time to express our feelings without causing harm. If you visualise pain as a build-up of toxic waste, at some point it has to be released, and if there is no outlet, it can seep into the land surrounding it. If that land is our body (and by extension our friends and family or work colleagues), then the contamination either becomes stuck or it seeps into other areas and causes *dis*-ease.

Like nature, there is an innate desire to self-rectify, but if the enabling conditions are not there, something else takes over instead. That something may trigger an auto-immune response or it may trigger a reaction. Either way, it can lead to far longer adverse consequences, for each time we ignore the warning signs, we pave the way for a pattern of harm to be reinforced. When that happens, the knock-on effect can have significant impact far further down the line, playing out sometimes years later. Pretending everything is okay is quite simply one of the worst things we can do. By ignoring the pain, we numb-out. When we numb-out we lose our innate capacity to care. When we lose our capacity to care we begin to cause harm, not just to ourselves but also others because we have lost our capacity for compassion. It's a downward spiral that has huge adverse consequences which play out at all levels within our lives, personally as well as at a business level. Once the loss of compassion sets in, sign-off of harmful enterprises on a larger scale becomes a new norm, especially in business and politics. It becomes a self-reinforcing cycle of destruction.

Expressing pain becomes intolerable and to survive, a wall – that is invisible but nonetheless there – stops any semblance of being able to feel. It takes increasingly high levels of personal or collective harm before anything is felt; the numbing-out has effectively prevented the brain from connecting with the innate.

Inner Ecocide

We all have inner ecocides that block our greatness. You know when they are at play because destructive habits, patterns and cycles come back to haunt you. They're easy to spot by the intensity of the feeling – the more upset we feel, the more entrenched our inner ecocide is – those personal harmful patterns, the old story that tells us we are unworthy, that leaves us feeling uncomfortable at best and downright awful at worst. Breaking the patterns of harm, luckily, is possible for us all.

Rocket Key

What personal ecocide is weighing you down that you are afraid to let go of? You might wish to try this one: 'I let go of my fear of speaking out.' Write it down (in your mind's eye) and beside you there is a rocket: open the door at the side, scrunch up your document and thrust it in, making sure to lock the door as you close it. This rocket's ready to go – all it needs is for you to press the button.

There behind a rock is a huge big box with a shiny red button on it – go, push it down. When you do – Buph! See your rocket launch out into the sky and burst into flames, showering sparks everywhere. Feel your weight lifting.

There comes a point in each of our lives, no matter what we are doing, when we decide to take our lives to a new chapter. Or life can determine this for us. Sometimes external events come into play, and often what seems to be a crisis can in fact be a moment that defines who we are. A moment of impact that leaves us stripped bare, when only something deep within can pull us through. Each person's experience of pain at the lowest point is nothing more, nothing less, than a very deep connect with the heart. Heart-pain, if not resolved, can sear like a cauterised wound every time it is reopened. To deny it is to disconnect. Deny it for long enough and we lose our capacity to feel pain altogether. Like layers of an onion, as we peel each layer the missing tears can come to heal the pain. Connecting with our pain consciously and with intent to heal allows us to break through the pain barrier and come out into a new space. I call that moment of connect a healing of our inner ecocide: feeling, healing and letting go. Sometimes this is the hardest thing in the world to do, but when we do, it can be enormously freeing. Each time we do it we let go of the trauma trapped within.

This needn't be a solo journey (we all hold trauma of some kind – a 'wound'). There are many experts who are far more skilled at working with trauma, who can create safe spaces for deeply distressing or disturbing experiences to surface and allow them to be met without blame. The Hoffmann Process is one of the very best in the world for intensive week-long retreats where trauma can be released safely.[8]

Facing our inner ecocides brings with it a growth in our capacity to feel – we get better at feeling and releasing our pain. As we move more into the space of feeling ourselves as bodies in motion, our emotions (literally, energy in motion) can rise to the surface with greater ease. Like bubbles trapped beneath, they can surface and be released and instead of experiencing an enormous volcano, soon the bubbles take on a smoother and more relaxed exit. It's like farting: the really big ones sometimes just have to rip, then the little ones come trippling through and they can be far less intrusive. The thing is, farting is energy too – and look how good it feels to let them out!

Fast-track Key

Go on, I dare you! Take time out to gift yourself some major inner ecocide feeling, healing and letting go. Want to fast-track it? Take a holiday in a beautiful place and do a retreat, such as the Hoffmann Process.

You may find yourself opening up to a whole raft of new experiences that change your world for the better. Then, afterwards, why not gift the same experience to someone else.

It is the innate being within us that tells us when we are feeling pain; it is our innate that tells us when something is causing harm. Disconnect from the innate and it becomes far easier to make decisions at a cerebral level that have the capacity to cause harm – another way of putting it is the heart and the sacred have been torn asunder. The innate is the capacity to feel, and feeling emanates from the heart. When we close down and lose our capacity to feel at a heart-level, then the heart has been energetically ruptured. When that happens, the disconnect is so great that corruption sets in. Corruption need not be lawful or unlawful to take place; quite literally corruption is the rupturing of the heart (consider the Latin words *cor* meaning 'heart' + ruption, from *rupture* 'to break') – heartbreak. Corruption can be viewed as a disease and you could say, therefore, it is treatable.

However, like many diseases that are based on disconnect (e.g., addiction, self-harming), treatment for corruption is dependent on the individual taking responsibility and actively deciding to change. For that to happen, either the person concerned takes the crucial first step into the unknown or external circumstances bring it about. Many who are suffering from corruption are either unable or unwilling to take that first step. Sometimes the greatest fear of all is the fear of letting go, even when letting go can pave the way for something better, and often those who are corrupt are very attached to control. So, how to break the cycle of harm? At a political level, as more corruption is shown to exist, a decoupling begins to occur. Societal disapproval collectively acts as a lever, as citizens no longer accept what is increasingly recognised as harmful. This creates a pressure point, where the cognitive dissonance is so great that something must give way. On an individual level, for the corrupt, that can be a moment of healing – a decision to stop. The window of opportunity opens to face the inner ecocide. Where that is not possible, enforced accountability can remove the person who is causing harm and give the opportunity for both the person and the receiver of the harm to enter into some form of process that aims to remedy the harm (known as restorative justice).

At a collective level, that requires law. But is there another way? Yes, there is. The more work we each do to heal our own disconnect, the more we contribute to the quantum field of consciousness. By breaking our own chains that shackle us, we break the chains for others too. As more and more people face their own pain and let go of the harm, the harm lessens for us all. Bit by bit, we each break our cycles of harm, so the harm is reduced elsewhere. One of the most powerful ways of being in service is to first heal thyself. It's not a quantity thing, rather how we develop our soul qualities – the more each one of us is capable of deeply connecting to our own pain, the more powerful the healing can be.

My Story: When My Inner and Outer Ecocide Met

I sat on the plane in agony. I felt it surge up inside me; my throat had a huge block in it, as if I couldn't release something deeper inside me. I'd just experienced some of the world's worst ecocides, and the enormity of what I had witnessed was searing through my body. I put on a movie to switch off, but all I did was cry. By the time I reached London, I was in a mess. My heart hurt. That night the pain was so bad that I checked in to A&E. I thought I was having a heart attack.

It wasn't a heart attack, but it was heart-pain. I'd tapped into something very deep inside of me. What was my inner ecocide, my shadow self, that needed to be expressed? Prescribed drugs did the trick momentarily, but I needed to do more to let it release. It was as if there was a blockage and I had to set it free.

What was going on here? There's a pattern of harm playing out – for me when I see ecocide, I feel pain. Only this time it's far worse. It's as if I am carrying the weight of the Earth on my shoulders. I have to let go of my belief that I must carry on alone and unsupported – I need support as I move forward. I realise that I have a choice: either continue as before or let go of my belief that I have to go it alone.

Healing

The more powerful the pain, the stronger the energy field. So, step back for a moment and consider this: when we deny powerful energy the chance to surge through us, are we not denying ourselves the opportunity to become something more? To go to the very heart of our being, to really pay deep attention when things seem to be at their worst can, if you so wish, be a conscious decision to go to the root cause of your wound – be it physical, mental, spiritual, or something else – and start the healing process. So here we have it; at that very moment when we feel at our worst, we have the opportunity to flip the switch.

Someone once said that 'emotional pain is a gateway into an energy wound' – and I so agree. Tap into our feelings and we step into a fast-track route to the very core of our blockage. Our upset is a red flag to say, 'Attention – something is blocked and requires to be sorted.' Our tears release chemicals to help our healing process.

At the core of most of our wounds is a prevailing thought that we are not good enough, that we are bad, that we've done something wrong. Most commonly it's a pattern of harm that has been learned as a child, when we are most vulnerable. By incurring the wrath or displeasure of another when we trigger someone close to us (most usually unintentionally), we unconsciously trigger unhealed wounds in that person and, in turn, we end up at the receiving end of their displeasure. That in itself can trigger within us feelings of unworthiness.

Most of us were conditioned to believe that it wasn't okay to express our feelings, even more so when our really strong emotions proved too much for those parenting us. Those who were our primary source of influence at a tender age, often without knowing it and without ill-will, closed down our capacity to feel and to express. That, in turn, literally turns us inward and we hold the newly formed belief that 'I am to blame/I am bad'. Next time we are scolded and the belief reoccurs, the pattern of harm repeats and embeds deeper into our psyche.

Part of the pattern of harm that comes into play is that we suppress the very fact that we are feeling pain. We pretend all is well, when sometimes a really good howl could make all the difference. But wait, 'that would be wrong,' says our retrained psyche. 'Don't cry, don't show, don't lose it.' We are ashamed to express how we feel in times of crisis for fear of being judged incapable of coping, both by the self and others. Sometimes our patterns of harm are so deep that a helping hand to support us along the way is all that is required. Seeking help is, especially for anyone whose hurt is buried deeply, sometimes the hardest thing to reach out for – and sometimes the very best thing to do. It takes huge courage to accept help, especially when we feel at our most vulnerable – and maybe one of the greatest things we can do in our lives is give ourselves the space to heal.

It is, if you like, a public service – tend to our own inner ecocides and others benefit too. As we each take the space to heal our own inner ecocides and move into a place of harmony, I believe we exponentially multiply the capacity for others to do the same. Not only that, as the exponential curve goes up, so too do the numbers of people who instinctively move out from behind their wall. As we dissolve our pain, the walls that imprison many others also begin to fall. Our own personal Groundhog Day plays out less and less. No longer do we repeat the same patterns of harm time and time again. With each one we resolve, so it becomes easier to face the next shadow that comes along. And if we don't take the opportunity, life very kindly obliges by sending round another.

Energetically as we face our inner ecocides, we raise our own consciousness around us and we effect one of the most powerful natural laws of all: the law of harmony. By healing our harm, we create the enabling conditions for harmony to take its place. And in so doing, by speaking our own truth to the power within ourselves that was holding us back, we stand ever stronger as we reclaim our biopower. Being energetically in that space frees us to be heard when we choose to step up and speak as a voice for the Earth.

The suppression of pain holds us back. Pain is there to guide us, to let us know that something is out of kilter. The more alert we are to feeling our pain and meeting it, the more aligned we become. The more aligned we are, the more harmonious we become and, like a finely tuned instrument, we become capable of playing a far greater range of music.

Pain lets us know we are out of key – there's a knob or two to turn to finely tune, but you know it when you are in key because it feels as if your whole world is singing. Keeping our inner ear closely listening for signs of flat notes and duff chords, so that we can get the tuner in when required – just as a pianist would do – or do our own fine-tuning as and when, keeps us free to play to the greatest of our capacities the rest of the time.

So, let those tears out; the best thing we can do is cry. Next time you see a child crying, go join them – encourage them to cry more and see if you can too. The child may be somewhat surprised to have a fellow howler, and you may end up laughing together instead, but hey, is that such a bad outcome? You may just have flipped the switch.

Harm to Harmony Key

Draw a line across a page. Map on it at one end 'deep harm' and at the other 'deep harmony'. Where it says harm, write your inner ecocides; where it says harmony, write your eco-joys.

Here are a few of mine.

Inner ecocides: self-doubt, fear of being hurt and a desire to be loved.

Eco-joys: dancing, sunshine and laughter.

Then take your pen and write, 'I choose to let go of my inner ecocides' and criss-cross each of them out. Then write, 'I choose to embrace my eco-joys' and circle them.

Another Way of Being

How come it's so hard to say, 'To be honest I don't want to do this/eat this/say this', or 'This really makes my heart sink', or 'I really wish I could do/eat/say something else instead'. Whether or not it's out loud or to ourselves, these statements can be a real challenge, especially when we have been brought up to do certain things, even when they are against our best interests. This can be particularly difficult when these things are for a perceived good, then we often feel bound by the thought that to speak out is to rock the boat. For example, my friend – a planning lawyer – really wants to create a new network around his community charters (see the website: communitychartering.org). Yet, he's repeatedly asked to draft planning appeals instead. Actually, many lawyers can do that, but very few have the desire to take forward the idea of community charters. Where do you think his skills are best put? Often when we are given the opportunity to take another path we are challenged to stay put in the same place. The greatness lies in self-discernment, to ask the question, where best to put my skills? One good indicator is whether others can step in instead. Ask yourself, who else is creating a new space with the work I am doing? If the answer is no one, or very few, then you are being invited to help create the new path. This is emergent energy – a dynamic that can create an enormous flow of exciting opportunities; people come forward to help and events open up. Bridges are created that suddenly take you on a journey you never knew was there. It's as if the universe is flagging up to let you know you are on the best path. Our senses become heightened and a delicious wave of joy comes with being in alignment with what we care about. Take note: this is really important (it wasn't in any of the textbooks I was given to read at school and none of the teachers talked about this) – being in the flow of an energy stream that carries you forward is one of the most exciting feelings to experience. It comes initially from the inside, not from the outer affirmation.

William's Story

William sat under an oak tree and searched within himself whether or not to speak about a cause that was very dear to his heart. Many had told him that to speak out would lead to rejection, social exclusion and certain detriment to his career. His was a choice point: stay on the same path or take another route. He took the latter. His decision changed history. In 1787, at the age of 28, he took a vow under the great oak tree to speak for the Abolition of the Slave Trade. At that moment, he made a commitment to give his all, no matter what it took, to bring to an end one of the world's greatest harms. What he decided set him and many others on a new pathway that changed the course of humanity.

Only you can decide what's best for you. Seek out what touches you deeply in your heart. If there is a greater vision of a better world that really **makes your heart sing**, listen to that calling. Follow that feeling of your heart singing and you will soon sense the route to take.

Of course, following our hearts brings with it the learning of a new set of skills – skills that cannot be simply read, they can only be learned by experience. How to speak with courage, how to face our personal ecocides and how to dare to be great – all of this comes about when we commit to a different route. This book can give you a sense of this but, notwithstanding what you read here, what really counts is whether you live it. That sense of being held back lifts when we shape our lives in accordance with what really resonates with us on a heart-felt level.

Once we know what we value – and that can change over time – and we give voice to that which matters the most, we are in effect creating our own life-path. What matters most to you? It needn't be something that's already out there – in fact the freedom comes in self-authorising, give yourself the permission to go and do something else instead. There is nothing worthwhile in being hidebound to something that does not bring you joy. If you feel that sense of 'I've got to do this, but I really do not want to,' then it's time to ask yourself: 'Am I free or am I chained by my own doing?' All of life is a choice. You can make seismic changes through giving yourself time out to ask: 'Is this for the best?' And you know when it is for the best because it feels good in your heart. **Tapping into the innate self** and having a deeper enquiry as to whether or not you are on the path that is best for your greatest self is one of the most overlooked, yet most profound steps each of us can take. Wouldn't it be fantastic if that was taught at school?

You could say that the innate is the smart part – the natural part that works from instinct to let you know what works and what doesn't. It's not the brain that tells us something on an instinctive level, our innate comes from a deeper sense of being – it's that part of us that knows when, for example, something is wrong, or when we are struck by love. Our innate has inbuilt wisdom, there to tap into whenever we wish. Even when we in our human state cannot see the bigger picture, our innate can.

Greatness also leads us to a deeper reliance on our innate sense of what works and what doesn't. The innate within us is a very keen radar – it's what guides us when we feel lost. The more we connect with the innate, the more we let go of any sense of being lost. And when we do that, we discover it's okay to not know what will play out next, and we are free simply to trust that there is something bigger at play.

Just by letting our innate self guide us, we become free of the need to control each and every step. Just as we walk without consciously controlling all the millions of cells, thousands of synapses and hundreds of muscles that are required, we can do the same when we decide to open up to our greater self – viewing ourselves as one part in a far bigger interconnected picture. Like pixels on a screen, up close the wonderful myriad of colours makes no sense, only when we view it from afar can the bigger picture emerge.

I have a friend who has a list, an **impossibility list** – the stuff that he says can't be done. This list he then sets out to disprove. What he's doing is challenging his own preconceptions of what is possible and that gives him a different perspective, one that opens him up to seeking out a solution. In so doing, my friend has let go of an old story that says, 'You can't do that, it's not possible', and instead he's replaced it with a different conversation that invites in the impossible as a friend. This frees him up to be more creative – he lets go of the sense that as a human there are limits to what is possible. It used to be said that it would be impossible to speak to people on the other side of the world, then someone invented the telephone; at one time it was thought impossible that you could see the other person as you spoke to them at the other side of the world, then Skype came along. Is it so impossible that one day we shall be able to travel in fossil-fuel-free pods that carry us across land

and water without causing harm? What about sourcing energy for free? Or better yet, communicating with people without the use of any technology or devices? Of course, all of this is possible – the only limits are whether we keep on asking the big questions that open up the space for the realm of potential to emerge. Open curiosity that translates into open questions opens the pathway to the new.

One idea that throws up many such big questions and impossible/possible notions is the **concept of energy**. A table is energy, just as much as we are. All matter is energy, the table simply resonates at a different frequency from us. When we view the world through the lens of everything being of one simple common denominator, our vision becomes more interconnected. Ultimately, our thoughts are an energy wave (and are recordable, just as the frequency of a rock is) – and when we set our intent, it is energy ready to be made manifest. Someone had the thought to make a table. That table is the tangible result of the energetic resonance of that person's thought. Indeed, all great ideas start from a thought.

Thus, it can be said that true greatness lies in the thought and the decision to take action on it, not the outcome – that the greatness lies in the person who gives form to the thought, which, in turn, creates the outcome. That outcome can be a table, a law, a cathedral, a painting and a gadget, or it can be how we decide to govern, how we undertake business and how we decide what matters to us. One person often starts a ball of an idea rolling, and others then resonate with the idea, helping to bring it into fruition.

A person finds a new path; it can then become a pathway that others can help to bed in. Sometimes those paths no longer serve us well. Therein lies an opportunity to create new ones. It's like a map without borders; if that path no longer works, create a new one and once a few more people follow it, you have the makings of a whole new map. In turn, the old map becomes a thing of the past.

I see a map emerging as we take our new steps; I know not where it will take us but I do have a sense that it is a world that is truly great. Working on the premise that our every thought is energy, then surely our thoughts made manifest become our map – a living map that grows in front of our very eyes. So, nurture those thoughts; you know the ones – ideas that emerge with the power to map out a way forward that makes our hearts sing. Nourish them as you would a good conversation with a cherished friend, explore them and give them space to expand. Take time out to have a conversation with yourself, maybe under an oak tree in an open space to explore the impossible, and dare to find the pathways that make the impossible possible.

Seek out the new where the old no longer works or has become stuck. To seek out the new is, after all, part of our evolution. Staying with what is, just because it is, only means that more of what is, is generated. Like a neverending loop, the same stuff goes round and round until the cycle is disrupted. One of the best things you can do is **to be a disruptive influence**. Being a disruptive influence for something greater than the self, cutting loose from that which holds us back, paves the way for others to carry the quest forward long after you have gone. *That*, I was not taught at school.

Tuning Into Happiness

There comes a time in all our lives when we ask ourselves: 'What in my heart of hearts would make me happy?' Cars, gadgets, property, status – you may or may not have all of that – but this is not what we are talking about here. You can have all the most exclusive trappings in the world and not be happy; you can have enormous amounts of money and still something is missing; you can have the top position and be fêted for many achievements in business but something more has yet to be discovered. I read somewhere that we read 100 times more news in a day than we did 100 years ago. Which means we have 100 times less space to reflect on our deeper needs than we did 100 years ago. As each year goes by, our lives become busier with so much more to assimilate: local and global events that do not directly affect us become secondary to everything else. Ironically, the ability to access more information has numbed us out. Especially when the news is a constant drone, deadening our nerve-endings and our inbuilt capacity for compassion. It becomes easy to turn off and tune out.

Happiness emerges when we re-establish our deep connect with each other. When we are happy, our creativity grows, we feel valued and we become far more likely to seek out shared responsibilities rather than shouldering burdens alone. We are innately drawn to help each other.

Disconnecting from community and those who live within our immediate surroundings severs our capacity to care for the collective. When our collective sense of being is restricted, we begin to shut off. Closing down the capacity to care is the direct consequence of the loss of our own sense of compassion. Somewhere along the way we have learned how to turn off and tune out. The problem is, this has a knock-on effect: we suffer and so does our community.

Decisions are made in isolation and it becomes easy to view each other as commodities; 'this relationship is not working – this person can be removed', can sometimes be a knee-jerk reaction to something that may indeed not work but could be met with compassion so that the parting of ways has less pain and those involved remain on friendly terms.

How easy it has become in this world to judge others as wanting and to be easily dispensed with, be it in a personal or professional capacity, rather than meeting each other from a place of peace. If anything, the hardest thing is to stop the inner critic that tells us we too are found wanting.

The blank canvas stands in front of you; what do you choose to paint on it? Do you choose to paint the most magnificent piece, of such beauty and wonder that it shall be looked back on in centuries to come as a work of art – or is your vision so limited that you prefer to leave it to another day? What if your vision of your own life is dull and grey? Would you not want to add colour and depth? Would you not want to completely rework it into something so great that you can only stand back and say with wonder – 'that's great!' So why not take a moment to explore in your mind's eye what you would put into the picture of your life.

But ... it's as if we are stuck on a TV channel we really do not want to watch, only it keeps on running over and over in our heads and soon enough we get sucked back in. We become passively obedient to what we see and what we hear; we have lost the will to object and instead, even though at some level it is very definitely not what we want, we continue nonetheless. There are millions of people who are sucked into jobs or ways of living they really do not want to be doing but cannot find a way forward. This one show is on repeat every day. To break the cycle, it must come from within: do we choose to switch the channel – or, do we leave it to the capricious whim of life? When we choose, we determine our fate, when we leave it be, we lose our capacity to be in charge. Either we change the channel or we remain stuck; the question is, what new channel do you choose, or better yet do you choose to let go of being boxed in completely and step up out of the box onto the stage of life instead?

Be it a film, a stage play or a painting – each medium allows us to explore what could be. By opening up our mind's eye to the world of potentiality, our ability to shape our own life improves. And the beauty is, because it's our life, if we end up with a picture that we want to change – yet again we can. This is one script each of us has complete authorisation over. We are the director, producer and the main star!

Turning Off Key

When you wake in the morning, what thoughts crowd in fast? Are they running in all directions? If so, step in and switch off. Think of one of those old-fashioned TVs from the 1950s where the picture has interference and has turned into lots of grey jagged lines on the screen. Reach over and simply turn off the switch. In its place open up a space for your focus to shift to something greater instead.

PART TWO

FROM SELF-CARE
TO EARTH-CARE

SELF-CARE

Stepping into the flow of greatness brings with it gifts – a new set of tools: insight, discernment, the ability to let go of the stuff of life that no longer best serves us, a strong inner compass and support. Each of these qualities are premised on our self-awareness.

Self-care is possibly our greatest challenge of all. It's so easy to neglect the self, to ignore the inner signals and patterns of harm. Time marches on, so much outer stuff boomerangs in that simply distracts us. Gifting ourselves even just a moment to check in and value our own ability to self-tune need not be onerous; indeed, it can be the one thing that keeps us on track. Our duty of care starts with the self – so go on, ask yourself the big questions (after all, this is a quest, so as the questor you are seeking out the best response).

Value Mapping Key

The ancient Greeks had two words for time: *chronos* (time) and *kairos* (space). One contains us, the other opens us up. Creating space in our lives for a deeper inner enquiry, where time is no longer the predominant driver, accesses creative freedom and pleasure. It's the space that opens up when we lose all sense of time and become fully absorbed in the moment.

Give yourself the pleasure to step into your space; if need be, put in your diary your 'sacred space' appointment. With pens, crayons and a great big piece of paper at hand, ask yourself, 'What are my values?' and map them out.

Allow those creative juices to flow, think big and great. This may be a document to return to time and again until you get to a point that you know it truly reflects all that you value and wish to take forward in your life.

Soul Qualities

We all have a unique combination of soul qualities. Those aspects of us that we can tweak from being good to becoming great. These are the ones to build on. Soul qualities come in many forms, they can be anything that comes naturally to us. For example, in one person it is the ability to seed humour into even the bleakest of moments, and for another it may be deep appreciation of beauty. Huge capacity for love, quiet support, loud cheering, the ability to lose yourself in a book, playfulness, strength of resolve, the capacity to envision the new – these and many more are all soul qualities. By having the insight as to what soul qualities we have, we can build on them and consciously bring them to the fore. Our strengths (another way of framing our innate soul qualities), when we recognise them and nurture them, can take us far. Not sure where to start? Try searching for an online strength test – one that gives you a series of questions with lots of different answers. What you choose leads you to your most predominant strengths. They can be a great tool for gaining a deeper understanding of the self and an insight as to where to put your energies – what's more, it forms a framework through which to recognise the strengths in others. The beauty of knowing is a freeing-up so that we can play to our strengths and where our strengths are less, seek out others whose strengths lie in different but complementary areas.

Bright Sparks

Like a multidimensional virtual electric circuit that connects up, down and sideways as well as through time and space, each of us is a spark – only each of our sparks do not disappear, instead each spark flows through the circuit. Each spark leaves a trail like a neon tail-light and each time we connect with other bright sparks, our lights burn even more brightly to ignite our pathways as we move forward.

The spark of greatness is one that cannot be extinguished, the stronger it gets the less opportunity there is for it to remain hidden. That's the thing – as your spark shines brighter you attract in other like-minded bright sparks like a magnet. Our innate being desires to meet others who are sparking up. So, the good news is, your journey takes you to places and people that match your spark. This means that as you step into your greatness, you'll find those you meet are doing the same. Like you, each spark shall be on their journey to open up the new pathways.

I have a funny feeling that there shall come a point when we shall look back and marvel at how far we have come. Sometimes, when we look back it's as if we are meeting a completely different person, and in a way we are. Who we were before may look similar, but our inner world has shifted and so too has our outer. As our inner radar begins to signal out that there has been a change in our state of being, so too does our life begin to shift in ways we could never have imagined.

Think Big Key

How big do you want to go? Thinking bigger than ourselves really expands the realm of potential – as big as the universe, maybe bigger. No longer are you focused on merely being a great person, you are now engaging with the big mass out there that has no definable end. Now this is big thinking!

Close your eyes, allow your mind's eye to take you out through to the edges of the biosphere, now go further, up past the stars and out to the outer realm, all the way to the furthest point you can reach. At that point there's a landing station; it's a special place, very beautiful, a paradise. You really like it. Take a moment to breathe in the beautiful scent and survey all that surrounds you. Notice the falling water and the seat beside it, there just for you. As you sit down you are joined by a group of happy beings who can help with any question you have. What a great place! It's a sacred space for you to connect with, and to tap into, your greatness. Your innate self loves it here – this is where the best conversations take place. Here's a space to ask the really big questions and ask for help.

Rewiring Our DNA

Just think, by daring to be great, how each and every one of us sparks off into an invisible super grid, building and rewiring our future paths, not just in this life but also other lives too. For me, I love the idea that we have many lives, not just this one – after all, it makes sense to many millions of Buddhists and countless tribal societies around the world, in places such as Siberia, West Africa, North America and Australia. Modern science cannot disprove this, nor can evidence be brought to bear to show without a doubt that we never return as humans. Indeed, many stories and ancient rites support the belief that reincarnation happens to us all. If that be the case, we can in this life set a path that can be carried through into the next. I love that. What we experience today informs our tomorrows, whether or not they are within this lifecycle or the next. So, think on this: by setting an intent in this life, consider how that can play out not just here and now but also well into the future of the many lives to come. We are only beginning to work out through quantum physics how our intent can shape time and space. And not just one person's intent; when many of us dare to be great no longer is it but one drop in the ocean. Very soon we have a ripple, then a wave, then a tidal wave – a sea of greatness – washing over many lives and touching many more. To return, having done the groundwork in this life, so that we can pick up and experience at an even deeper level what it means to be great the next time round sounds like yet another adventure in waiting. Is it possible that we are rewiring the very DNA of our bodies so that we can contribute something not only in this lifetime, but also for the lives of many more to come, should we choose to do so?

Check-in Key

You may sense, as you journey along the path of greatness, that it becomes increasingly difficult to say something that is a fabrication – whether it be a small fib or a huge whopper – to the point that you feel discord. Do not worry, this is your innate alerting you to an energy drain. When your energy of greatness depletes, you become more alert to the absence. It seems that there is a direct correlation between energy depletion and how you feel, and indeed there is. Not being in a state of greatness can be felt and sensed.

By now your senses are becoming more in tune with your greatness. Being out of sorts can range from a niggling feeling that all is not right to feeling sick in the pit of our being when we act out of turn. This is the alert signal – by sensing whether we feel energised or not, it taps into the innate self to inform it of an imbalance. If it doesn't feel good, in all likelihood it is not the best step to take. It may only mean that there could be another route not yet explored. Take time to ask some questions such as: 'Is this for the best? Right now? If not, later? Is there another way?' Check-in and see what it feels like. Does this action bring to the forefront a sense of 'Yes, this feels right', or does it sit uneasily with you? Dig around and ask questions from different angles; that's the way to get to the bottom of the unease. It may be that there is a fear there – maybe it's about releasing what is holding you back instead.

Not feeling right about something is sometimes the best indicator we can have to pay ourselves some attention, ask some questions and get in touch with our innate.

Tools for the Journey

You're now ready to set sail. But this is the thing about daring to be great. When a great ship is in harbour and anchored, it is safe, of that there can be no doubt. But that is not what great ships are built for.

When we build a house we begin with the foundations; the upper floors shall be solid and secure only if they have been built on something unshakeable – same with a great ship. Before you leave the harbour, let's pack in some tools, to be pulled out as and when, so that you can sail even the stormiest of seas.

Tool: Language of Care

Our words can create disconnect. Could it be that the very language we use with each other sets us up? How we phrase our intent can call in conflict – and worse, war. Words like 'conquer', 'campaign' and 'discipline' are all war words. All too often we 'fight against' something or we call the other side our 'enemies'. We are opposed; metaphorically we're 'up in arms' about whatever issue we disagree with. By using the language of war, we set up our own disconnect: us versus them – the unknown enemy. Energetically this is exhausting.

Take this situation: we have the evidence that whatever we object to no longer works – an injustice is clearly at play. What do we do? Set up a fighting campaign, but it takes years to resolve, and even then what little remedy there is, it's too little too late. However, we can approach injustice in a different way. Meeting harm need not be a fight. There is another route, based on open transparency. It's an invitation to engage in accountability. Yes, the harm can be proven to exist by the bringing of evidence and yes, that process is in itself important. But where do we go from there? If the harm is not recognised as a crime in law, then there is no leverage. Shining a light on a harm through a court system ensures a proper hearing can be had. When we do that, and invite in the opportunity for those who are causing the harm to take responsibility, we can collectively begin to find new pathways forward. Simply fighting against a harm without some route to accountability is all too often a basic re-enforcement of a pattern of harm. Creating accountability (and a court of law is one forum) and giving name to the crime opens the door to putting in place a process to bring to court a perceived injustice and to find remedy. Without it, we are left disempowered in the face of conflict, resorting to fighting with our words.

Tool: Self-Authorise

The concept of self-authorising our lives is a very non-Western concept. Yet, it's one skill to add into the toolbox that helps us along the way of a life without pain and suffering. By choosing to self-authorise, we let go of the nagging worries that hold us back. We free ourselves to fly as high as we wish. The only permission needed is our own. Permit yourself to be the greatest you can be.

Whether or not the critical voice comes from within you or from others, it matters only that you take a step back and ask whether you wish to believe it. The voice that says, 'You can't do it' or 'You can't say that', 'You have no authority'. Rubbish. It's your choice as to whether or not you accept restrictions in your life. A life in greater freedom lies ahead – all the barriers in the world are in your head and are illusory. Our fear is not what we don't do, it's the fear of what we can do when we step into our own power. So, I dare you to let go of the fear – better yet, you can say, 'Stop. I've had enough, no more'. Do that and you will discover you can, and you do, have authority to say and do whatever you like – you have your own authority. Only you choose to cede your own self-authority to others, and only you can choose to take it back. Self-authorise your life and, instead of waiting for someone else to give you a mandate to speak or do, take the initiative and be confident that you will be supported if it's for the best.

Know this: a life in greater freedom brings with it greater mountains to climb, greater oceans to sail. But by climbing the mountains of life and sailing its seas, you become a master of the art of adventure.

Two routes: two very different approaches to life. Do you choose to self-authorise your life or do you simply sit back and let others determine who you are, what you do and where you go? One is participatory, the other passive. In the first you are the driver, you are in charge of where you go; it's a life of conscious transformation. Sit back, however, and the world around you determines your fate. It's your choice; self-authorise or accept the dictate of others (and the critical voice within saying, 'You can't do that' can be one of your inner dictators).

Tool: Setting Intent

You can say it, write it, chant it, draw a picture of it, sing it – whatever gets your intent out there. Why? Here be three reasons:

1. Intent is energy not yet made into form.
2. Giving expression (voice, vision) gives your intent form.
3. By giving it form, your intent has moved to an outward expression that sets in motion something tangible.

Energy and motion moves forward. In quantum physics what you have done is moved atoms of energy with conscious focus. Where they go next is up to you. You are in charge – literally, you are charged by the energy you have just put in motion. You can now determine how best to use this new energy. Life will afford opportunities; some may not seem like opportunities until later but if you catch them as they come, like a feather in the wind, then there's your chance. Remember great moments can be known sometimes only to you; sometimes they are seen by others too – it matters not who sees them, but whether or not you are willing to step into them. Windows open, so go climb through them – remember there are no fixed rules. Enjoy.

What you have done is, through the use of intent and the giving expression of it, entered into a different mindset – one where you are the master of your fate. You get to determine your life. There's a difference here between reacting to life and responding to life. Reactions are in opposition; responses are in flow – a stepping into the opportunity. We all know when we have reacted badly to something, it can leave us feeling deeply uncomfortable. We also know when we have responded well: life is joyous, we feel lighter, with less baggage and more space to engage with the challenges we meet.

Tool: From Intent to Manifest

We say one thing, set an intent, then Boom! Our intent gets overridden; in come random or conflicting thoughts. This is radar clutter – the stuff that stops clear intent becoming manifest. Our radar has gone off-kilter. So, let's clear our radar clutter, to make sure the pathway is straight so that when our message is sent it cannot go off target and miss the mark.

Setting an intent sounds simple, but in truth the art of a good manifest lies in being clutter-free. Buddhists call this stepping into the void, entering a place where there is a moment of space. It is here that an intent can be set. Another way of accessing it is through sleep; set an intent just before or after sleep when your brainwave activity has slowed down.

Like archery, steadying our line of focus to the exclusion of all else, the arrow of intent lands in the centre when the two connect. Any distraction can bring the arrow out of line. To keep focused on the end result requires a clear vision and a sense of the present. Being present to the intent being set prevents diversions from coming in, and anchors the moment when the vision has taken shape.

Imagine you have a vision of, say, what the world shall be like in twenty years – it's a beautiful vision, abundant with nature flourishing, many trees and biodiversity. So, you wish to set the intent for this to happen; however, while you are envisioning this you remember that you must go and buy food for dinner. This is radar clutter. A random thought floats up and skewers the vision. Time to clear the decks, get back to the open space and fill it with your explicit intent; you take charge of what enters the space and by being alert and focused on your vision the intent can be set. But – and this is a big but – vision alone is not enough.

There is another step: action. Without actioning the vision, it remains just a pipe dream – literally stuck in the pipe instead of flowing to where the windows of opportunity open up. Manifesting is a proactive endeavour, yet so many sit back and wait. And wait. And wait. But remember, you are in charge, you have created the vision, you have all the help, keys and tools around you to make it happen. All you need do is take action. 'Action without vision is only passing time, vision without action is merely daydreaming, but vision with action can change the world.' Thus spoke a man who really did change the world: Nelson Mandela.

Manifesting is simply the art of intent made physical. Whether that be a wish for a new car or a wish for humanity as a whole, what matters is the clarity of the intent. Be sure of what you wish for, give yourself the space to envision it and ask whether it is for the best. If it's not, there may be another route that is for the best (different car, different global vision). What is your vision of how you live? What is your vision of your own health and wellbeing? If, when we think about it for a moment, we can really manifest our future, then surely one of the best things we can do is get dreaming.

You are life. Your thoughts can change the world.

An Example of Bringing Vision into Being: Bastoy Prison

What if our justice system put in place something altogether different instead? What would that look like? Would we have prisons that no longer have barbed wire and instead have open grounds where inmates are given the opportunity to participate in growing, connecting with the land and each other, where the new norm included exploration of what had caused the inmates to inflict harm? Such a place requires a shift in our thinking about how we perceive criminals – if embraced, instead of punished, a form of restorative justice takes place. One of the recurrent themes within the reform system is that there is very little reform; often those who are imprisoned are given scant support and as a consequence end up reoffending time and again. One prison that has taken a radically innovative approach is Bastoy Prison in Norway. Bastoy has done away with physical boundaries; it is an open prison, no walls, just trust. Prisoners are given opportunities to learn new skills, mainly outside (remember, this can be a very cold country for six months of the year). An assessment of each person's strengths ensures that what is already there is built upon.

Collaboration and community are actively fostered. Of course, there are consequences; should you choose to walk away and not honour the contract, you are placed back into the conventional prison system. Not one person has walked away.

One man held the vision for a prison where people are valued: Arne Nilsen. He is a quietly spoken yet firm believer in the potential to reform justice by valuing the offender. And he's doing it. What he has done with Bastoy Prison provides a model of what is possible.

First steps are often like that: take a vision and bring it into being. Others very soon begin to tap into the same vision and build upon it. Part of my vision of an end to ecocide is ultimately for a world where we no longer need prisons at all. That's not to say we abrogate our responsibilities and let chaos reign. No, what I am envisioning is a world that individually and collectively takes responsibility, and where there is an exception to that new normative, restorative justice can come into play. The space is created for both the parties to meet, with the aid of skilled mediators and a process of exploring how the pattern of harm can be broken begins. By taking responsibility, the perpetrator can initiate remedies. Like the Bastoy Prison, if the opportunity is missed, the perpetrator is given help until that time when he or she is ready to face their responsibilities. This may take a very long time for some; for others it may be far faster. The timespan is not what matters here – it's the high level of support. In other words, it flips the conventional prison system, which is based on a command and control model, to a model of accountability and support. The majority of persons entering into the new model find their own lives becoming aligned with their sense of being supported and trusted, thereby having a knock-on positive effect for society as a whole. Does this sound like a pipe dream? Maybe, but it's working already in Norway.

Tool: Plan Your Demise

'Plan your demise' is a wonderful idea that was introduced to me through Rob Hopkins, founder of the Transition Town movement.[9] It used to be how many ancient cultures lived. Working with the premise that we are only here for a short period of time, and therefore we can choose how best to use our time before we go, speaks of legacy.

Just imagine you have stepped into a room where you meet someone you truly love and they say, 'I'd love you to have the greatest life possible – but here's the thing, you get to choose what that will be like. By the way, you have all the time in the world – until you die. So, what is your legacy to be?' Okay, you might think, 'Who do I choose to be?' This is the clean slate, this is it, I can choose to be anything I want – but wait – 'I choose to be great and if I choose to be great then I shall surely leave a legacy that is great too. So, I choose to put in place something that shall have lasting impact once I have gone, something that shall contribute to a greater world long after I have left.'

For some, ours is a journey to be continued. For others, it's a one-off. Either way our life, at this moment in this place, is something to treasure. Gandhi said, 'We shall pass this world but once. Any good we can do, therefore, or any kindness we can show to our fellow human beings, let us do it now because we may never pass this way again.'

Looking far ahead, way beyond the life of now, frees us of the fear of death. It's as if we have been transported out of our bodies and have the capacity to experience the future as we choose it to be, long after we have gone. How far ahead do you dare to explore: next century, 2,000 years hence or bigger yet?

Tool: Nourishment

Observe the lifecycle of a plant: see how a tiny plant can grow in the most inhospitable conditions, even pushing up and through concrete in cities. No matter what, plants seed, germinate and grow despite the lack of nourishment. The most crucial time of all is the nurturing of a seed into life and as the seed grows into a plant, nature attracts others that can give support. The key moment is when the plant bursts into life; earth, sun and water provide sustenance so that life can take grip in even the most hostile of terrains.

So, too, do we require nourishment. Physically, mentally and spiritually. Look carefully to the self: all too often we deny our needs in the face of what we perceive are greater needs – the destruction of the Earth, enormous acts of violence and war, extreme poverty in other nations. I learned this the hard way: my body would give way underneath me so that I would be forced to stay in bed. The world would spin and I'd lose track of time and space. Only this was a trip I really did not enjoy – yet, like Groundhog Day, I journeyed there many times before I chose to put myself first. I'd work 14- to 18-hour days for weeks on end, I'd sleep 4–6 hours at most, without any time out. I'd get to a point where I felt as if it took all my strength to keep on going, and always there was more to do. Then one day my legs gave way. As soon as I stood up, I'd collapse. I needed a rest.

It makes sense to optimise our conditions so that by the time we leave this world we leave a legacy that contributes to the greater whole – a legacy of our own choosing, one that speaks of our intrinsic values and is a fuller expression of who we are. Like nature, it takes a diverse habitat to help the little seed of greatness within us to flourish, and so too like a plant do we require to be nourished. Nourishment, of course, comes not only from food. Nature understands the wisdom of companion planting – the diversity of plants that enhance each other's growth. Where do we choose to plant ourselves? Is our community mutually supportive? Are we nourished by our surroundings? To be powered by our Earth community is to be hooked into a system that gives energy as a constant renewable source.

How we physically connect with the Earth, the very soil beneath our feet and how we connect with the life-source we receive from each other, feeds us. Our community need not be geographically determinative (although it really helps); what matters more is whether our companions have similar values.

Tool: The Power of Story

Civilisation has changed direction many times before – and when it does, the winds of change blow in. Humanity has a far greater capacity to adapt than we accept as possible – we face change all the time. However, for some the safest route is to stay put, even when we know in our heart of hearts it does not work.

Just look at how fast we accepted the norm to be sitting at a desk all day long, staring at a computer. A century ago, the image would have been deemed insane. To step into a food shop where most of the food comes in tins, packaged and processed or wrapped in plastic, instead of being fresh and local would to a nineteenth-century shopper be nonsensical; to fear that what we eat may or may not be tainted by pesticides – or genetically modified – was not even a thought that existed before the middle of the twentieth century.

Change, when it comes, comes fast – but whether it serves the health and wellbeing of humanity and the Earth is debatable. What is more recent is the human lack of response; if anything, humanity has become domesticated to such an extent that our ability to break free and speak out for something greater when we see a harm playing out has become dramatically lessened. So, let's change the story – and let's change the laws to support our new story, a new story based on the greatness of humanity and the greatness of each and every single one of us to stand up and speak out for what our hearts yearn for, to live life in greater freedom.

'George Banks' was a man who understood the power of storytelling. As a man who during the daytime was trapped by a job he hated, George would spin tales of great adventure for his kids especially when poverty struck each time he was sacked. The family would be forced to move on, from place to place, seeking some way of making ends meet – it was a precarious existence, and George was not a man best placed to be sitting behind a desk all day, every day. His mind craved a very different world. This man was a dreamer. His dreams are best known through the writings of his daughter, who brought alive something even bigger. Hers is a story with a better ending than the one that befell George Banks, who died an alcoholic. Her father was vilified in his life for his creative tendencies. In her later years, she wrote his story from a very different perspective, and the story was one that spoke of an incredible greatness – a man who brought to his children something far more valuable than money: hope.

George's stories, written up by his daughter and given a new breath of life, have been read by children across the world. One man in particular was so taken with them when he read them to his children that he spent twenty years persuading George's daughter to let him make a film. Her fear was that her father would be portrayed in a poor light instead of being honoured for what he stood for. What she wanted more than anything was for her father to be redeemed, rather than judged badly.

White society of 1914 Australia was fraught with a belief in status. All the trappings of prestige were outward indicators of success, a wife well dressed, a good job, a big house and servants. A man with little or no interest in such a restricted life was scorned. A man who dreamed of adventure, magic and the impossible did not fit. But George Banks was honoured; he was redeemed and all he stood for was saved.

Not in his life, but in the imagination of millions of people in the world today.

He was a man who dared to express himself differently and value life differently – and the legacy that has come from that continues on. His daughter learned the gift of storytelling from him and she used the power of stories to reframe the world and give it a greater sense of hope and it is this notion of hope that sits at the heart of the greatest stories.

It's a story known to millions; you probably know it too, it speaks of change and hope, not just now but time and time again. The real-life George Banks was in fact Travers Robert Goff, the father of P.L. Travers who gave birth to the wonder of *Mary Poppins*.

There is a sense that change is blowing into our lives right here and now, only we get to write the storyline of what happens next. Like P.L. Travers, we are faced with the same choice: we can look back and decide whether we carry forward a story of harm, or whether we choose to put in its place a new story based on something greater instead.

Sometimes it's painful to look back on times past, especially when our cultural circuits have long told us a story of ecocide. But what if we choose a different story? A different view can give a radically different interpretation. It can free us up and we can let it go. It takes courage to revisit painful memories of the past, especially the ones we've buried deep. Looking back can open up wounds that have never properly healed; the fear is that the memories will trigger the trauma, but mercifully that needn't be.

We can claim a different life and by remembering and choosing, we can let go of the fear of the past. Honour your past it's what shapes you now. Look back and know that your story is a truly great one, and each chapter is a stage that brings you to who you are now.

Freedom Key

> You are a bird, soaring above all that is around you, being able to view from afar. You've caught a thermal, it's allowing you to simply glide smoothly and peacefully. The air is warm and comforting and the view is magnificent. All you need do is give an occasional flap and let your wings spread as wide as they can and allow yourself to float. Look around and let whatever you see shift your perspective.

My Story: Meeting My Past

I meet myself aged 7; she's skinny and shivering – just been swimming in the cold waters of the west coast of Scotland. She seems upset – I'm not sure why. Higher up the sand dune, on a wild and windy outcrop, I can see my mother and grandmother sitting together; the rest of my family are nearby. I wrap my arms around her to warm her and I tell her not to worry, that she is to have a great life and that I am so incredibly proud of her. I tell her how she will help create a new law that will bring an end to so much harm.

She runs back smiling, I know she will be okay.

Some Choice Recommendations

Only do it if it makes your heart sing.

Choose to let go of anything that causes harm.

Challenge any negative thought that creeps in.

Be open to the impossible.

Ask big, open questions.

If in doubt, ask yourself, 'Is this for the best?'

Seek only your own permission to act.

Be open to the passing opportunities and the unexpected.

Share what you learn.

Let go of the outcome.

EARTH-CARE

What are the tools we can call in to assist with the patterns of harm we see playing out globally? You might think that existing tools are not enough to prevent and disrupt our existing norms. What do we have? We have over 500 treaties, conventions, protocols and resolutions specifically pertaining to the environment – yet none of them is supported by an enforcement mechanism. The law is missing.

Where there is no enforceability provision in a criminal court of law, there is no accountability. More than that, the state has no legal duty of care to act on behalf of its people. Without the support of new laws, we remain disempowered and hidebound by old laws that no longer work.

It's not just one tool that is required. In fact, what is emerging is a whole new body of law called Earth Law. Lawyers and non-lawyers across the world are connecting and advancing Earth Rights, Ecocide Law, Community Charters and applying Natural Law principles to how we govern our lives. The same principles are being voiced in other spheres and there is a cross-pollination. Lawyers and non-lawyers are meeting to explore how best to take forward new tools. Ecocide Law sits at the heart of the body of Earth Law; its heartbeat is a new beat, one that beats strong. And, one that is growing stronger every day, each time someone picks up this book.

Ecocide has three iterations: ecological, cultural and personal. The draft Law of Ecocide is for ecological and cultural ecocide – prohibiting significant harm at a collective level. Identifying our inner ecocides gives us the choice as to how we individually choose to self-govern.

How we govern ourselves is just as valuable to the whole of society as are the laws we put in place to govern the decision-making of those in a position of 'superior responsibility' – CEOs, directors, Ministers of State, financiers – and hold to account in society.

Tool: Law of Ecocide

In the Ecocide Act, ecocide is defined as 'extensive damage, destruction to or loss of ecosystems'. When we care for the Earth it makes no sense to commit ecocide; ultimately we all suffer, both human and non-human beings.

Most commonly understood as ecocide is ecological harm – often it is visible, such as the destruction of the Amazon. Cultural ecocide refers to the damage, destruction to or loss of a community's way of life – both ecocides are premised on a wider expansion of concern for the Earth community and our relationship with all beings.

The common thread when an ecocide occurs is the lack of care; whether it be an action or omission that is caused with intent, recklessly or without knowledge – what is known as the *mens rea* (the state of mind) is irrelevant. It is the consequences that occur, or could occur, that are prohibited. Why is this so? Because most ecocides are not deliberate. Most CEOs do not willfully decide to destroy; profit is the driver. Where there is intent, it counts as an aggravating feature.

The occurrence of ecocide – the absence of care and the causing of significant harm of our Earth community – is dependent upon the creation of law that names ecocide as a crime, as opposed to a mere civil breach. There is a difference: civil laws seek to give remedy for a harm (by way of payout), whereas criminal law seeks to break the pattern of harm by prohibiting it. Civil law does not necessarily remedy the wrong caused at source (the company can continue as usual), whereas criminal law can (a person is held to account in a criminal court of law). The power of criminal law is the power to prohibit, prevent and pre-empt certain acts that are no longer acceptable.

Tool: Creating a Legal Duty of Care

In legal terms, business as it is set up today has, through the use of ownership laws, sidestepped an overriding legal duty of care. Instead, the number one duty has been to put the interests of the shareholders first. Thus, demand for profit takes precedence over considerations for health and wellbeing of humans and non-humans. The consequences of there being no international laws to stop companies from putting profit above people and planet are enormous. In addition to human-caused ecocide, the increase of catastrophic events highlights the lack of a fiduciary duty of care not only in business but also in politics.

There is a world of a difference in law between an owner of a property and a trustee. Put simply, an owner can destroy or cause harm to his property without being held to account. A trustee, however, holds in trust – often land – that which he or she has been entrusted to take care of on behalf of beneficiaries for both current and future generations.

By law, a trustee must put the interests of the beneficiaries first; this is termed a 'fiduciary duty'. When the beneficiaries do not benefit, then the trustee has failed in his or her fiduciary duty and can be held to account. Should a trustee destroy what is the life-form of the trust (e.g., the land), thereby bringing to an end the benefit, that trustee has in law failed in their duty of care. A business owner, however, can destroy the life-form of the contract (e.g., the land) and thereby bring to an end the benefit, yet where there is no legal duty of care, little can be done.

Clearly, the legal relationship determines the outcome. As an owner you have very little responsibility to that which you own and even less to any others; as a trustee, however, you have a legal duty of care, often to others you may not even meet in your lifetime.

In business, ownership prevails. And so, where a company has contractual rights over a territory and destroys it as a result of pursuit of profit (such as for fossil fuel energy), there are virtually no rules in place to stop the damage, destruction to or loss of ecosystems. At an international level at the moment, it is not a crime during peacetime to destroy vast tracts of land – and yet, during wartime it can be a crime.

Compare this with community land projects that are set up on trusteeship rules. Unlike business, community land projects have a legal duty of care, which means that health and wellbeing principles take supremacy. So, in legal terms, broadly we run business on ownership rules rather than trusteeship rules, which in turn leads to a lack of duty of care for the community affected and a lack of taking responsibility for current and future adverse consequences. Moreover, business – like politics – is run on short-term returns, thereby mitigating against planning for the longer-term. Neither politics nor business has an overarching legal duty of care to put the interests of the wider Earth community (in which I include not only humans but also all who live and are inhabitants of our Earth) first before profit. Thus, communities across the world every day suffer significant harm for want of fast-gained financial returns.

Earth Trustee Key

Stepping into our greatness takes us up a gear. It's a step onwards from care for the self to care of the wider Earth community; a relationship – our relationship – with the world expands. Our cycle of compassion has extended and now our duty of care has become all encompassing. To be an Earth trustee is to ensure the health and wellbeing for future generations.

What does that mean to you? See if the following statements resonate for you and if not, explore what does: being my purpose, caring for both people and planet, trusting my innate. Then have a look at the bigger picture: global harmony. What does that mean to you? See if the following statements resonate for you and if not, explore what does: Earth Law, human responsibilities, rights of future generations, peace.

There is great power that can be harnessed through the pursuit of greatness. I talk here of the power to effect greatness within our lives that contributes to a greater world, a world where we are ecocide-free, free from our inner ecocides, and free from cultural and ecological harm.

Creating enabling frameworks, be it through the creation of law or the setting of intent (for creation of law is one form of setting of intent made manifest) is an essential aspect of how we move forward. What are the enabling conditions each and every one of us requires to flourish? Put a group of people in a camp surrounded by barbed wire and withdraw their right to their land and you will find that those people very soon begin to suffer.

The community can no longer live in greater freedom, and as a result begins to break down. The same thing happens when we surround ourselves with barriers that prevent our freedom to think big – the voice that says, 'You have no right, who are you to speak?' These are barbed words indeed, and in accepting them we no longer allow our being to be free, in greater expansion in thought and action. We become imprisoned in our own smallness.

Just as in law we have Enabling Acts[10] – acts of law that cut through the chains that hold progress back – so too is it sometimes necessary to break with convention so that a greater freedom can operate. We too have our own enabling actions, or practices, that empower us to move forward. More than that: when we break our own chains that bind our mind, we create a greater freedom not only for ourselves but also for others around us. When we shift our own terms of agreement, those who do not agree tend to move away, creating more space for others to radiate in who are aligned with our new state of being. In turn, our world begins to operate on a different level, one where we choose what happens next. Our world begins to constellate events and circumstances that meet our intent. Now all that is required is for us to take action.

The Sacred Trust of Civilisation

There is in law an ancient tenet that dates back in writings to the sixteenth century. Often overlooked, it nonetheless is encoded in the first charter for the United Nations. The original wording makes explicit our overriding duty of care to all beings – not just human beings. It is the language of trusteeship law. By 1945 the wording had been narrowed down to a limited remit, applying only to territories that were officially designated to be former colonies now named Non-Self Governing Territories (NSGTs). Nevertheless the principle here, of putting first the wellbeing of all beings, remains.

Set out in Article 73 of the United Nations Charter:

Members of the United Nations which have or assume responsibilities for the administration of territories whose peoples have not yet attained a full measure of self-government recognise the principle that **the interests of the inhabitants of these territories are paramount, and accept as a sacred trust the obligation to promote to the utmost,** within the system of international peace and security established by the present Charter, **the wellbeing of the inhabitants of these territories.**

In law, a trustee's duties are based on the equitable notion of conscience and conscionable conduct. Prioritising of personal, professional and business interests are improper; what comes first are the duties of service to ensure the wellbeing of all beneficiaries. The trustee must act on behalf of the interests of the beneficiary, not for its own interest. Therefore, for the purposes of the sacred trust of civilisation, we are the trustees who are bestowed with the position of responsibility: we have a fiduciary duty to the beneficiaries of the trust asset. The asset to be administered by the trustees is the territory, and the beneficiaries are the inhabitants.

Thus, a sacred trust is both a state of being and of doing, which when adhered to prevents the abrogation of the universal value of the sacredness of life. The very use of the word 'sacred' underlines the importance such a trust is accorded, reinforcing the moral as well as the legal obligation it imposes on all.

A sacred trust is premised on two values: the sacredness of life and our interconnectedness. I believe we can bring the sacred trust to the fore by placing it firmly at the centre of our world. Written law is one thing, what we adhere to within ourselves is another. Can we put at the heart of all we do a sacred trust? I believe we can. When we value life itself, something fundamental shifts within. Our ability to embrace a world of peace is suddenly attainable.

Article 73 of the UN Charter has wider implications for how we engage with civilisation as a whole; a sacred trust need not only be for the few – at the heart of it lies the belief in the supremacy of a duty of care that applies to everyone. Each of us counts, and how we choose to action a duty of care for humanity and the Earth is up to us.

Holding to Account

Holding to account sets in place something that acts as a check and balance. To be counted is to matter, to be valued. Accountability is the ability to be included, to be answerable. The notion of answering for our actions arises from the origins of the word accountability – 'answering for money held in trust'. The basic premise is a trusting one and where the trust is broken, we are held to account for our actions.

Decide to commit ecocide at a collective level, and you are held to account in a court of law. To simply overlook a harm is to remain complicit; however, to hold to account is to stand fully in our belief that we all count and the actions that cause harm, or the lack of action to prevent a harm, are no longer lawful.

Criminal law flips the burden of proof. But it goes further than that; by creating a Law of Ecocide no longer is it acceptable to say that ecocide is needed (for profit, jobs, etc.). It is not a defence to say a harm is a good harm. In the eyes of criminal law, what is determined is whether a harm is occurring. When evidence is brought to the court, it matters not that it is justified on economic reasons; what matters is whether the harm is so significant as to amount to an ecocide. Fines are not applicable to international criminal law (remember it is individuals who are held to account first and foremost, not the company or corporation). By way of analogy, take the example of a CEO of a publishing business running the defence against pornography and trafficking charges, that they should not be convicted because many people's jobs depend on it. Their counsel would advise the client they have no defence in law. Apply this same situation to a CEO of a company running the defence against ecocide charges – likewise their counsel would advise the same.

Criminal law in effect changes the story of our times. No longer do we buy in to the justification of ecocide as a valid harm. Instead we choose a greater story – one free from harm.

The Bigger Picture: Claim, Name and Frame

How we claim the space and frame the narrative shapes the outcome. Often when it comes to contested issues, it becomes a warlike zone: does peak oil exist? Is fracking safe? Is GM harmless? Whether you listen to the companies with a vested interest and much money to pay PR representatives and commission reports that back their claims or whether you choose to undertake some due diligence yourself – either way you may end up completely confused.

Who to listen to? Well, maybe you do not need to be an expert to determine where you personally stand. Ask yourself: is this for the best? Is it for the best to continue drilling for oil with ever more adverse consequences? Is it for the best to drill underground and pump down vast quantities of chemicals underground? Is it for the best to modify genes?

There is a common thread here: does X cause harm? If so, it makes sense to stop. You need not be an expert to determine whether a significant harm has occurred. Just look at images of ecocides across the world, such as the Athabasca Tar Sands, mountain-top removal, deforestation of the Amazon – the harm is visible to the human eye in these instances. It is a crime to harm a human, but when it comes to our Earth, we have yet to put such crimes in place. Which means that abuses on a major scale have become accepted as our norm. Just as slavery was accepted as a norm because it was not a crime for a long time, so too is ecocide.

But also like slavery, public disapproval is escalating; communities adversely impacted by their ecocide are speaking out. People across the world are becoming increasingly proactive in showing their support and where local communities are not being heard, their stories are being shared across social media in real time. It becomes harder and harder to hide. Individuals are taking it upon themselves to connect into an alternative media that portrays a very different story; proper reportage, rather than repeat-age. Choosing to be discerning in our newsfeeds, rather than accepting the norm, is in itself an opening into a whole new story. Often this new story directly counters what the mass media says. Which takes us back to our starting point: does X cause harm? And if so, is it a significant harm?

A Law of Ecocide sets out parameters of size, duration or impact. They are guidelines only, as every ecocide is unique. Just as we do not have checklists to determine whether a human has suffered grievous bodily harm (GBH) or actual bodily harm (ABH), there are some cases that are clear cut and others that fall into the grey area. Case law builds and is used to help a court determine whether the harm is so significant to be a GBH or the lesser harm of ABH.

We do not, as of yet, have an international crime of ecocide – whether or not we choose Ecocide Law is up to 'we the people'. Do we choose to end the era of ecocide? To stand up to what seems an enormous weight of force that keeps an existing system in place is a great challenge. Which is why I believe it shall take greatness to put in place Ecocide Law and if we are to call on our political leaders to be great, then surely it becomes our duty to be great too. Those leaders with a strong moral compass have already seeded in them the kernel of greatness. As do each of you reading this book. So, let's lead by example – and name our ecocides. Harm with no name remains hidden.

This is our land. It's up to us what happens next. How we choose to claim the space is up to us. View the Earth as a thing and it simply becomes a commodity that can be bought and sold without care for the consequences.

But view the Earth as a living being and we embrace its intrinsic value, not the imposed value – the very sacredness of life. Instead of 'I own' we shift to 'we owe a duty of care'.

It becomes a collective responsibility, not just for here and now, but for the lives of future generations too.

Care replaces commodity. Costing nature tells us that it possesses no inherent value; that it is worthy of protection only when it performs services for us; that it is replaceable. In one fell swoop, we demoralise and alienate those who love the natural world while reinforcing the values of those who don't. We remain stuck in the cycle of harm.

Claim the space. Not as an owner of your patch of the Earth, but as something far greater instead: as a trustee, a guardian, a protector. Instead of harming our home, let's put in place a duty of care.

Often law plays catch-up with where civilisation is; it took the aftermath of the Second World War for genocide to be given a name; it has taken much more for us to get that point where we can say 'this is ecocide'.

Frame the narrative. How we choose to call in support for Ecocide Law is important. We can be raging bitter, fighting against the injustice – or we can come from a place of deep care, seeking restorative justice and a better way of preventing future harm. Ours can be a vision of a world where we have ended the era of ecocide – a world where we harness the power of the sun, water and air to provide the alternative to conventional fossil fuels, a world where we no longer cause significant harm to the Earth, culturally and ecologically. A world where we are protectors (not protesters), speaking from a place of care and upholding a system of decision-making where a 'first do no harm' principle is paramount.

By framing the narrative in terms of a better world that adopts a Law of Ecocide, investors shift their perspective:

mining and extraction of oil becomes a risky venture, looming laws that will prohibit dangerous industrial activity, such as mining operations/pipeline proposals/deep sea drilling, mean that what was previously the norm is no longer viewed as a secure financial investment or trading commodity. Long-term investment signals flip: with Ecocide Law, it no longer makes sense to put money into what is soon to become an illegal activity.

This is our legacy. What we choose to do next opens up a space for something greater to emerge. It's up to us – together we can claim, name and frame.

PART THREE

CREATING A MORE BEAUTIFUL WORLD

I SEE A WORLD WHERE WE HAVE ENDED THE ERA OF ECOCIDE

Ours is a time of change. What that change is – is up to us. How we govern ourselves is first and foremost what sets us free. How we govern our society comes next, and when they are aligned to our intrinsic values and our search for greatness, our laws give us the most powerful bridge of all. When that bridge is crossed this is what I see.

My Story: My Futurecast

I'm looking out across a valley, fertile and green. I can see below me groups of homes that are very beautiful; local materials have been used as well as plants to create clusters of living Earth buildings. Each home is inspired by nature, with big windows and light-filled interiors. They're heated by air-source, ground-source or solar heating. Those who are close to water also receive energy generated by community hydro-share schemes. Food is grown locally and shared by the community.

As people travel, vehicles are far quieter and the sound of nature prevails. Further afield, transport infrastructure has changed beyond all recognition; there are now super-efficient networks right across the country, and the trains are a delight to use. On-train services include fresh, organic food made daily at local hubs, there are swivel chairs in the floor, and ceiling viewing galleries for socialising and enjoying the views, and more intimate spaces for those who wish to rest. Our train stations are busy community hubs, beautifully kept with edible plants to graze on, and they are warm and hospitable.

Cities with car-free zones have the best infrastructure of all; this whole new kind of train transport is the preferred option due to its low-noise, no-emission, top-comfort appeal. Everywhere you look is green; nature has been brought back. Roads are lined with trees and plants. Birdsong and butterflies fill the air. Everyone seems so much happier now that the 'three-day working week' has become the norm – those who choose to remain work-free are given free housing. People say they are more content and quality of life is what matters. Work is far more fluid; more and more people skill-share and swap homes when they go travelling.

Trust is the basis of many transactions and money is used less and less. Schooling is no longer in one place; as families travel more, so do children, and schooling has become far more centered around values and experiential play. Different cultures share their space with young and old alike. Health and wellbeing are a given; many more people self-care, and it shows. An older generation has fewer illnesses now than ever before and a younger generation is growing up breathing and seeing without the need for drugs or glasses. The water is so clean that it is safe to drink straight from rivers and canals, the air is no longer filled with pollutants, the soils – even in the cities – are no longer depleted by pesticides, which have become a thing of the past. Government as we know it no longer exists: sub-governance, bio-region by bio-region, has replaced centralised government and makes decisions from a 'first do no harm' principle, which has obviated the need for much planning and regulatory law. The health and wellbeing of all beings comes first.

Ecocide Law has been passed in every country, but by the time this happened, due to the five-year transition period where every company was given help to switch, very few prosecutions were taken. A few companies were closed and a few individuals were found guilty, but they have all accepted responsibility and have entered into restorative justice hearings. Enormous restoration is underway in many countries and borders have been removed so that communities can easily support each other's restorative work. Land is being restored, communities are being rebuilt and primary assets – community land trusts – are given top priority. Transport, health and energy now cost far less, with some of it being free. Communities are flourishing and life itself, of both people and planet, comes first.

Prisons are becoming a thing of the past as fewer crimes are being committed and fewer prisons are being filled. Instead open facilities, where inmates learn how to grow plants and food and engage with nature, take their place. Big institutions are rare now; smaller localised and networked hubs of diverse skill-sharing are taking off, and there are great people helping set them up. It's so much easier to tap into global events and to communicate. Many more people are exploring the next generation of conflict-free technologies including air-bound transport and WiFi-free telecommunications. The internet has changed beyond all recognition – no one has laptops now – the ease of accessing information for free is a given and we no longer use wireless (or wires) to transport signal. Far less complicated systems are in place now – even a 7-year-old child knows how to connect up with her chums in a different continent without a computer!

Arne Naess, the great Norwegian ecologist, who coined the term 'deep ecology', believed that when we think from a place of a greater duty to the Earth community, we then create much that is of beauty. He spoke about 'thinking dutifully, acting beautifully'. Our sense of duty, he reasoned, came from a place of deep care. From there all that we do can only be beautiful. It becomes impossible to do anything that causes harm – not just to other humans but also to the wider biotic community. To destroy our Earth simply makes no sense. There is no beauty in mass damage and destruction. A beauty born of deep care, however, is a beauty that comes from the heart – not simply an adjunct, added on as a veneer.

Here was a great man aligned with natural law – he looked to nature to learn and he spent vast tracts of his life deeply connected to the Earth, in particular the mountain he grew up on. His ideas radically shook up the world of academia and he became the youngest professor at Oslo University where he introduced values-based teaching as a prerequisite for all students when they first arrived there. He greatly encouraged his students to explore big ideas. For him, to think dutifully was a necessary prerequisite to all that he did – be it having fun with his students or speaking out on ecological issues.

Charles Eisenstein's book *The More Beautiful World Our Hearts Know is Possible* explores the idea of beauty too. In it, he touches a chord within – what our hearts know is possible is radically different from what our heads put into the old story narrative. Had we listened only to our heads, laws such as Genocide and Apartheid may never have been born. Those were laws that were born from a deep sense of our duty of care for humanity. Expanding our sense of duty into the realms of what Charles and the Vietnamese Buddhist monk Thich Nhat Hanh refer to as 'interbeing'[11] – the interconnectedness of all beings – expands our sense of self-care to Earth-care.

 ## My Story: Late Majority

It's been a great talk and I can feel the audience really support Ecocide Law. Many are keen to hear more. There are lots of questions afterwards and people linger late. Copies of my second book, *Earth is Our Business*, are selling well. My fellow speaker turns to me after the event and says, 'Yeah, but this is never going to happen.'

It is as if someone has pierced my heart. A million thoughts race through my head. Being defensive, scathing, angry, upset – none of these reactions help. This guy just didn't get it.

Then a friend turns to me and says, 'Don't worry Polly, he's a late majority.' She's right – he'll come on board, but not yet.

Building Bridges

People who really get Ecocide Law tend to be open to ideas that are real change-makers – they have a gut instinct response. For others it's a real challenge, even for those who care. Everyone wants to express their opinion, positive or negative. If I had followed those of a negative disposition, I would have closed up shop and gone home a long time ago. The only way I could stay the course was to listen to my own heart. In my heart of hearts, I know that Ecocide Law is for the best. I cannot square it with my conscience to stop speaking about what I believe in, but initially I couldn't understand why some got it when others didn't.

Simon Sinek wrote a book that unlocked my mystery, called *Start With Why*.[12] In it, one diagram in particular fired up my synapses. His bell curve, called the 'The Law of Diffusion of Innovation', completely substantiated my own experience and showed me how I could move forward despite the moments of despair upon meeting others who were in a different place. What he gave me was a profound insight.

My natural instinct was narrative-based; here is a law that has the power to change the world – but how to get this one big idea out there? I was used to legally advising; being a campaigner did not work for me. This narrative, I felt, was a powerful lever for others with campaigning skills to put to good use. There was a better path to take here, one where I decentralise and cede any ownership, thereby letting everyone take this law forward in whatever way they best saw fit – could that be the way to bridge the chasm?

Simon Sinek shone a spotlight on the importance of bridges; he talks about what it takes for an idea to make it in business as a success. The same applies here. For me, Earth is our business so his take on an uptake of a big idea – whether it be Apple Mac or, in my case, the Law of Ecocide – fitted. There seemed to be a chasm between those who are big thinkers and those who needed something more before they would come on board. Simon Sinek names those who think big, 'the innovators and early adopters'. Those who need the reassurances of their peer groups are what he calls 'the early majority' – they come on board when they see others they trust as being supportive. Here was another insight: those who don't get it at first are capable of moving, often all they need is to hear the idea from peers they trust. So, the innovators and early adopters say, 'I'm with you all the way'; the early majority ask, 'Who's already on board?'; and the late majority people say, 'Yeah, it'll never happen'.

The tipping point – the point that determines whether an idea will fly – is the bridging of the chasm between the early adopters/innovators and the early majority. It's one thing to get many innovators and early adopters on board, another altogether to bridge the space and have the support of the early majority. So, how to 'cross the chasm'? If it's not crossed, the early majority will not come on board until someone else that they know or trust has endorsed it. The innovators and the early adopters, they've got a wider comfort zone – they're comfortable going with their innate. Innovators and early adopters listen to their gut instinct and are driven by what they believe about the world; not by what others say. Theirs is a self-governance that is internal, not external.

'The first two and a half percent of our population are our innovators,' according to Simon. 'The next thirteen and a half per cent of our population are our early adopters. The next thirty-four per cent are your early majority, then your late majority and your laggards. We all sit at various places at various times on this scale, but what the law of diffusion of innovation tells us is that if you want mass-market success or mass-market acceptance of an idea, you cannot have it until you achieve this tipping point between fifteen and eighteen per cent market penetration, and then the system tips.'

So, the tipping point for Ecocide Law is far smaller than you might think. Our market, if you like, is people who care. It has to be said, not everyone cares about a Law of Ecocide – but that's okay, the objective here is to create the bridges so that those who do care come on board and help tip the balance.

Those people who can bridge the chasm are the ones who can help effect most change. Each of us, I believe, can be a powerful bridge; reaching out to others who seek assurance from elsewhere. It means reaching out to those who are not yet sure whether to listen to their innate.

Building bridges brings together some unlikely alliances, it opens up new cross-pollination, and gives permission to others to come on board. Bridges can also be events – platforms for seeding big ideas, especially platforms that reach out to the innovators, the early adopters and the early majority. Ecocide Law is one big idea ready to spread.

My Story: One of Those Tipping Points

Three weeks before the US elections I ask, 'Do you really think the US shall have a black American President?' It was an exciting moment. I wondered how many times Barack Obama had been told, 'This'll never happen'. That's precisely what some of my friends said too. Obama must have heard other people's doubts countless times. Without letting it pull him down, he held his vision.

Here was the first-ever black President of the United States and suddenly it was a new norm that everyone accepted.

Suddenly everyone had shifted. I had an insight: the tipping point for Obama came far earlier, when the chasm between early adopters and early majority had been bridged.

Treading a Greater Path

You know when you are really onto something great when people tell you, 'it's impossible'. Just imagine how many times Obama as a young black man must have been told his dream was unrealistic when he declared he'd one day be President of America, just imagine how many times women were scorned and told that it was unimaginable for them to have the right to vote, just imagine what it felt like to challenge a prevailing norm in times past. Be it colour, creed or sex – how we govern ourselves and society is shaped not only by what we consider acceptable and unacceptable but also how sometimes all it takes is for one person to hold a vision of what's possible, and then taking it to others to join in the new vision until the tipping point is met. That person, if there is true belief in the vision, may just change the world. The path chosen is a different one, even if he or she has no idea where it will go.

I remember hearing a quiet gentleman speaking at an event where all the other speakers before him had given their extensive list of credentials. He didn't do that. He told a story instead. He spoke about his career in marketing and how one day he turned up at his office and thought, 'If I disappeared tomorrow nothing will change. Someone else will simply fill my space and the accounts will be sorted.' He wanted his life vision to be so much more than that. He walked out there and then, and his life changed forever. He chose to go explore a very different path, not knowing where it would lead. Now he is a famous author in the US.

One of my all-time heroes was a welder in the Scottish shipyards of Glasgow who dreamed of playing music professionally. He had a moment where he chose to make this dream a reality. He was asked whether he was going to take the leap – he was playing nights and working days – why not jack in the welding and make a life out of what he really loved? When he replied that he'd maybe do it in six months, his old chum said, 'You'll never do it. If you really wanted to do it, you'd quit right now.' There was an uncomfortable moment, then his friend spoke from the depths of his own longing, 'There's nothing worse than being an old guy in here, knowing you could have gotten out when you were younger.' That Friday, our welder walked out and never returned. His gift to the world was telling jokes and strumming a banjo.

Dream Key

Are you living your dream? Take a moment to dream the life you'd love to live – what images come to mind? Imagine stepping into what you see, take time to explore and see how it feels. If you find yourself saying, 'I'd love that', you know there is a dream that you can make into a reality.

Living life in greater freedom is a life of choice. Rather like free-form dancing, the steps we take to get there change all the time. The people we meet along the way are sometimes there to help or there to deepen our experience or commitment in some way or another. When we view fellow travellers along the way as helping us on our journey, it becomes easier to step out.

I love meeting people who have defied convention in some form or other and have taken up a life that many others would never in a million years consider. My friend – let's call him Angus – lives off the land and has forsaken wearing shoes for nine years now. Occasionally he turns up in remote Scottish newspapers, seen walking barefoot in the snow. He tells me it only took a season to reacclimatise to the snow and that it is us, in our air-conditioned, centrally heated buildings, who have become un-acclimatised. He seeks the freedom to live life treading lightly on this Earth and yet police stop him and arrest him on spurious charges because he wears no shoes, lives off the land and has no form of written identification. Some might scorn him, but I feel that Angus, more than anyone I know, has found a path that is in alignment with his values. As he walks, he talks to all he meets. His is a message of treading lightly on the Earth. Some people get it, others find it a threat. What matters most of all is that he is living life the way he wants to, without causing harm. It's a different kind of conversation – one with no end.

This is true not just for Angus, but also for you and me. To converse is an art form, an ebb and flow, with many turns. It's an invitation to come with, not a demand. A conversation about greatness seeds an idea that can germinate and grow, linking present to future and back again. Letting go of any cultural circuits that hold us back frees us to plug in to a greater open source. And when we do, we invite in a whole new way of being – creative, in harmony and with care. It brings with it a willingness to express and shine a light where others may fear to tread; seeking ways to courageously go forth and speak as a voice for the Earth.

What we choose in life as our values can be revisited at any time. Our moral map has no borders to confine us. Each of ours is different and just as we are unique, so too is what we choose. The pathways remain hidden until we step out, opening up with every step. How you chart your journey over the seas of life is up to you – sometimes the best is a light hand at the tiller, with a tweak here and there when you feel a little off-kilter, sometimes something more is required. Whichever route you take and however you chart your course, remember this: by choosing to dare to be great, you choose a challenging path. It's one being explored by others too, so invite them in to share it with you.

Being Open to the Windows of Opportunity

You know that moment when you catch a passing comment and you think, 'Yes – I can do that.' Sometimes these moments are fleeting, but when they arrive they have the potential to open up our world to a whole new perspective. It can be something someone said, or a thought that pops in, or even an overheard suggestion or conversation. What matters is not how the opportunity presents itself; it's the recognition that a window has opened with the opportunity to fly out with the winds of change. We can stand on the side or we can open our wings. Often these openings are fleeting, to be taken when they arrive. Life seems to be like that – it's not something to park for a rainy day. Surfers get it – no point letting the great wave pass you by when the ride is calling. When the moment comes, when that wind of change gusts through, like that bird riding the thermal, enjoy soaring high. That moment when you feel the caress of the wind is the very moment to take the leap.

A window missed will swing open again until we see it for what it is. Sometimes the opening holds little promise at first flush – but hey, suspend that closed thought for a moment. Let go of the thoughts that hold you back and look to the essence of the message. Do you feel a sense of 'there might be something in this'? That's your moment. Listen deep, not just to what you hear, but also to what you feel.

Someone you barely know says, 'I know someone you should meet.' Do you act on it? Well, what does your innate tell you? Do you feel that sense of 'yep, I'm gonna do this because it feels right', or does the brain come in and say, 'ach, it's probably not going to work' or, conversely, do you sense that it's not right? That's an equally important response. Check in with your innate – the sensing part of you – and you'll find stepping into the flow becomes far easier, unbiased and unhindered by the brain. It's often our brain, not our innate, that overrides our best decision-making mechanism, thereby frustrating our ability to take the opportunities that we have in fact invited in.

So how does this work? I set an intent and if it's heard, then it seems that my world conspires to find the windows to fly through. What you intend has its own field of attraction – so when we dare to be great, life meets that intent by putting in place opportunities for greatness to be explored. However, making explicit our intent is not enough.

There is a second part. It's no use putting out an intent and sitting back and waiting for things to come to you – being open to the gift, in whatever form it takes, is key. Which reminds me of the story of the man whose house was flooded: he set the intent to be saved by God. So he sat on the roof of his home, surrounded by water. A helicopter came – but he refused the lift, saying he was waiting for God. A boat came by, but no, he wanted God to appear. Same thing happened for three days – he kept on turning down every boat that came by. When he died, he asked God why He never rescued him. 'I send people to save you,' God said, 'but you didn't let them help you.' Four times he missed a window of opportunity, all because he didn't think it was God. That's the thing with setting an intent, don't get hung up on who comes along to give you the lifeline.

From Radical to Cutting-Edge

An idea whose time has come is an idea that refuses to go away. Yes, it may be radical for a short while; for a time it uproots our way of thinking, but then something shifts as it takes seed and we get used to the idea. How long it takes for a radical idea to uproot our existing frame of reference depends on how fast it spreads and how widely it is seeded. Now more than ever, our capacity to spread ideas is enormous. Our avenues of communication today are far more democratic than ever before; now everyone can have a say. So how long until a radical idea is no longer radical?

My Story: An Idea Whose Time Has Come
A British newspaper got in touch very early on wanting to do a double-page spread. It was to go out that weekend in their Sunday magazine supplement. 'Great,' I thought, 'this will really seed out Ecocide Law.'

I open the paper and it's not there. 'Sorry,' I'm told, 'but your idea is too radical. Our readers will want to know who else supports it.'

Sometime later, I get a tip-off; my work is turning up all over the place and the editor has had a rethink. It ends up being published in all its glory. The journalist drops me a quick line: 'Just to let you know – Ecocide Law is no longer radical, it's just cutting-edge.' It took four months. Something tipped there; not sure when, but it did. Maybe, just maybe, the same will happen again and again until the scales of justice are completely tipped, and Ecocide Law is put in place.

How Big Are Your Dreams?

Nobody, I'll wager, believes in their heart that the really great thing is to always make sure other people come first. I'm not convinced that the epitaph 'She always put the needs of others first' is a great one. That would be to deny our own needs. Where is the greatness in that? Yet, look around you – how many people do you know that are denying their own needs (the need for support, the need for sleep, the need for time out)? How many people are tied in by jobs that suck? Or jobs that end up in extreme burnout? Or jobs where the needs of others in a far worse state come first? Or jobs that generate extreme levels of stress? Or jobs that are a huge mismatch for them and their skills? Or jobs that end up being abusive in some form or another? All of this and more, yet it seems impossible to step off for fear that everything will come crashing down.

What precisely is being sacrificed here? A life? And for what? Yes, there may be bills to pay and mouths to feed, but what are your needs that are being denied so that others may flourish? Is this how it's supposed to be? No. Our own ecosystem is massively out of kilter if our own needs are being suppressed. So, working on that basis, if we look around us, you could say that the majority of the people in the world working in offices day in day out simply to make ends meet, and to meet the needs of the firm/the government/the charity are denying themselves the right to life – to flourish and be nourished. Of course, there are companies that are truly great to work for – and if you are working in one of them, fantastic. But what to do if your own needs are not being met? Especially where you have become a slave to a system that you do not believe in.

Ask yourself this: how big are your dreams? What is your dream life? I had a friend who worked in a mediocre middle-management job for a bank in the city; it was a dull job. One day she went home and sat down and wrote her own obituary from the perspective of where her life was. It was not inspired. Then she wrote another obituary, this time with all her greatest dreams of what she wanted to be. It changed her life. She left her job, gave up her flat and off she went to follow her dreams. Her life is an adventure and, of course, with that comes many challenges.

I have a theory that within all of us is a deep yearning to be free, to follow our dreams and find the greater purpose of our lives. Somehow, we've become incredibly domesticated – like animals that were once wild, and are now tamed. Why is it that the wild speaks to us at such a deep level? I think it's because it touches something deep in our cellular memory, a recognition of the greatness of that freedom. We've closed down our capacity to go off and re-wild for fear of what it may unleash. Yet, look to the wild – it flourishes. Domesticate a wild animal or bird and something closes down; have we become so tamed that we are unable to access the wild spirit in us that wants so much more? If anything, our capacity to think big and be great has been trained out of us, boxed in by the walls of our lives. A wild animal does not choose to be caged, so why on earth do we accept it in our own lives? We talk about thinking outside of the box, but this is about getting rid of the box altogether. Nature has no straight lines, so why do we surround ourselves with the linearity of grids when we could step into the non-linear, emergent and wild?

When each of us opens up to the deep yearning within, to live life free – a life governed by only our innate sense of being – only then do we truly discover how to fly.

GREATNESS AS A LEGACY

Steering a New Course

A great friend of mine shared his story with a group of us around a dinner table one night. He was a diplomat. What happened could have cost him his job, and also his life.

He was, he told us, stationed in a country that punished anyone who spoke out against authority and often resorted to killing them. Word got to him that a very dear friend of his had been badly beaten up, tear-gassed and was refused treatment because of her political beliefs. She had spoken publicly about environmental injustice. Violence on the streets and riots were escalating. Shootings were the norm.

My friend took a diplomatic car and drove to the hospital to find her, knowing that by supporting her he could be expelled by the government, leaving his career in ruins. He found her beaten and badly bruised, but far from defeated.

She was in such pain and shaking so badly that she could hardly hold a pen that was in her hand. On top of a page she had written the following letters: GUINAO. She could barely speak, but she said to him, 'Promise to live by them the rest of your life'; it was almost as if she was giving him a farewell message – 'GUINAO means Giving Up Is Not An Option'.

Sometimes powerful words come from others when they are least expected; words that express so much more than just how a fear has been overcome; words that speak of deep commitment. You know when it comes from the heart because the fear of the self is trumped by something greater. My friend's story did not finish there; he bundled her up and took the leap – instead of leaving her there, he barged out of the room. Something had to be done, he had to take her to a safe place, even if it put his own life at risk. He knew there were men standing outside the room with guns, ready to shoot her. But leaving her there was not an option. Amazingly, he got her out alive. My friend had in that moment acted on behalf of something greater than himself – he knew that this woman needed help. The woman was Wangari Maathai, the first African woman to win a Nobel Peace Prize.

I have heard stories like this in many different forms, but they are essentially the same – people in extreme circumstances step into greatness for the sake of something greater than themselves.

Each of us has the capacity to step out and do something great. Choice points happen not only at times of risk of injury, harm or loss of human life, but also at times of mass damage and destruction of our Earth.

Legacy Key

If you were to awaken and be told whatever intent you choose today would leave a legacy for the world that puts in motion events and consequences far into the future, would you say, 'That's not for me – thank you, but I'll stay in bed' or 'Wow – let's give it a go?'

In fact, everything we do has a ripple effect and can change lives. The bigger question is whether or not those ripples effect a greater change for humanity as a whole. Maybe the best starting point is to ask whether it's the greatest we can be. And not just in the here and now, in our immediate surroundings, but also whether what I choose to be creates, or could potentially create, greatness elsewhere as well, for many years to come. Does it make sense that I set in motion something that could take me on the greatest adventure of my life? More than that, could it lead to world peace? That to me sounds great.

When we truly believe that we can make a difference and are committed to effecting great change, giving up is not an option. If anything, it's those moments of crystallisation that drive us forward each time. When we are committed to act, the setbacks drive us forward to an even higher gear and the refusal to let go seeds within us a strength that cannot be surpassed. Every step we take, even if we do not know where it will lead and even when it's a setback, is a step that takes us to a very different place.

Being in service is a conscious decision to effect great change in one's lifetime, for the greater good. How that is done arises out of the commitment. We all have unique gifts – everything we require to help us discover what our exceptional gifts are can be found all around us. It's just that it's not always apparent. How often has it been that with the benefit of hindsight you have looked back and said of something upsetting that it was a gift in disguise? Have you ever felt pushed when you did not want to move, and yet now you see that it was very much for the best in the larger scheme of things? The challenge is to let go of the sense that whomever did the pushing acted unjustly; to bear the grudge is to remain enslaved to the desire to punish.

It used to be thought that leaving a legacy was only for the realm of kings and popes. It's not a title that determines legacy; each and every one of us leaves a legacy. A legacy that is truly great, however, speaks of fearlessness in the face of opposition, taking action – even when in fear – for something greater than the self, standing up and speaking out even when no one else will, setting a course that brings humanity closer to peace. That is a legacy that we can all commit to. It's also a legacy without attachment to outcome; for the long-term results may never be seen or understood in our lifetimes.

Legacy to me speaks of intrinsic values made manifest. It is also for the future; what I can do in my lifetime so that, long after I've gone, many of those whom I shall never meet live a life in greater peace. What do I choose to bequeath to the future? What is my legacy?

Great Ideas

Start with a great thought and take the first step. Each step we put in place leads us to the next one. Simple, you might think, but think again: in fact, each step can be leading us to a completely new destination. Or, we can choose to remain in a wheel, like the mice that run round and round and round and round. By stepping off the wheel and putting trust in the unknown, the path opens up as and when we need to see it. Maybe the freedom comes in not knowing – instead allowing our purpose to determine where is best to go. That's a great step, letting go of the need to know. Once that step has been taken and the intent is set to be open to the unknown, then the magic begins.

By inviting in the sense of being in service to something greater than the self, we each dare to be great. There is a direct correlation – between the something that is greater than the self and our own greatness as a human being. In fact, to be in service to greatness is to be willing to let go of anything that holds us back from ceding control over our own lives. And if we accept there is something greater than the self (of which we are part of), to meet it is to embrace the greatness within ourselves. Greater freedom results from the breaking of the chains of our inner ecocides; it is our restraint that tells us that we must first make sure that we stay put. If anything, when we allow ourselves to go to the edge – that place where we step into the unknown and act from a place of courage – we enter into a space where very different terms of engagement apply. No longer are you restrained: you are free to think big.

This is no small feat; by coming out from our controlled lives (and stepping out of our comfort zone) we invite in many new challenges. But instead of seeing challenges as something to fear, I invite you to name your shadow as they each rise to the surface, let them go and move on. Each challenge we face is our moment when we can choose to take charge and release whatever it is that binds us. Like an onion, with every challenge we meet, we peel off another layer. As each layer is shed, we come closer to the heart. We move into a space of deep connect.

Collective intent fast-tracks a great idea; as each of us takes responsibility for our own state of being, so too we see it reflected out into the world. No longer is it tenable to continue living in a world of ecocide. Breaking the chains one by one, we step out into a freer world.

 ## *My Story: My Community*

As I sit here writing, the sun sets across a beautiful valley nestled in the midst of the Cotswolds in England, where much of the farming that remains is organic or biodynamic. Community Supported Agriculture, a thriving farmers' market, ecological businesses and active groups dot the surrounding countryside.

I have chosen to live here, near Stroud. Stroudians have a radical approach: theirs is a community that speaks out and takes action, bound by strong beliefs and values that shape who they are and what they do, especially when their land is under threat. There is a sense of collaboration and support.

The story of Stroud and the surrounding Five Valleys is not one single narrative but an evolving one, as many people give voice and make visible their values in many ways, with a strong vein of refusal to sit by and passively accept the 'what is'. Instead, this is a community that is striving towards something far greater instead. What is so wonderful is that there are so many burgeoning communities around the world just like here, where people are coming together with common intent to make their world a more beautiful place, one where the very health and wellbeing of all beings matters most of all.

Being in service to something greater than the self is at heart a realignment. During this realignment, entrenched commercial values are set aside and a fundamental shift occurs in how we view our world as we step away from money being the goal to money being the tool, to be used instead to support our dreams, not the other way round. This is not to dismiss money, but to see it for what it is as a tool – a physical form of energy that we can choose to put into effecting something greater.

By stating our needs, we can call in the support we require. When we manifest our needs, we find that others step in to help. Help comes from unusual sources, rarely from the place we expect – and that applies to money too; when it is gifted with conscious intent that comes from a place of freedom, then something magical occurs. All the help and support we wish for is truly there.

Our energy shifts each time we say 'no' to old energy; by saying no to an old mindset, we free ourselves to be open to new pathways. Old rules no longer apply and money for money's sake no longer works. Give it a try – put the manifest first and see what happens!

Live Life Free

One last thing: are you clear about what you want to manifest – what it is you want to happen – before putting out the ask? Then ask your innate: is this for the best? If it doesn't feel right, let it go. When it comes to money, invite it in, from a place of greatness, nothing less. It's there to help, not shackle us to that which we wish to do. Oh – but here's a thing; when help comes, make sure to celebrate!

Our outer world mirrors the collective inner world; it's a participatory endeavour to change it and we can each play a part. Look all around you: it feels good to be surrounded by people who care about you and whom you care about; it feels good to look out and be nourished by a green and fertile land where our water, soil and air is toxin-free – this is our world, a planet of choice. So, too, is our inner world. It feels good to dream big. It feels good to dare to be great. Our inner landscape is echoed in the world in which we wish to live, so it can only be that our world will one day be free from ecocide. 'Why do it?' you may ask. 'Why live life free?'

Because it's a great place to be.

I KNOW

Please read this at the celebration of my life.

To all my friends:

In the event that I die sooner rather than later than I plan, I ask for all my friends and supporters to hold a huge party with festive fayre, much dancing and music. I ask for the great work to continue. And I know it shall, for the seeds have been planted and all that is required is for others to sound the horn. I know my work is done when others start to call in greatness too. So whatever way I die, please celebrate life and all its greatness that is vested in each of you. It is my intent to depart as and when is for the best. Should that be at an early stage, please be reassured that this is for the best and I have agreed to it. Our lives are for the choosing and I choose that my life be one that can serve others, even if that includes departing early. I have to say, this really has been a truly great life and I am filled with great joy and happiness to have met so many of you – each one of you has helped as I have followed and sometimes led in this life. We each give boost to our lives when we let go of fearing death. I know that I am safe, and I no longer fear my own death. I know too that it is simply a passing from one life to the next and I know that our paths shall cross time and time again.

I love this land, this Earth. I love the wondrous experiences I have had. I love the gifts I received. I love the joy I have had, especially since I have moved to Stroud. I love the community here, the deep care for nature and humanity that I experienced. I love my gentle moments at one with nature, such is the beauty of this place. To experience first-hand what it is to live and connect to people and planet that are in harmony has been for me the best party of all. My life has truly been rich.

I know this shall be read after I have gone, and so it is that I can leave this message with you: I leave this world knowing it is already a better place. I know I have played a part to help that happen, and I know you have too. I know it may not yet look like it, but we are sowing the seeds of greatness for countless generations to come. That is the Great Work of our times. Yours and mine.

Polly Higgins
Friday, 10 October 2014

AFTERWORD

by Dame Jane Goodall

Our current environmental crisis is not something new. I remember saying some years ago that the concept of 'ecocide' was long overdue and could lead to an important change in the way people perceive and respond to the fact that we are destroying the natural world. Indeed, in many places we are using up natural resources faster than nature can replenish them. We are in the midst of the sixth great extinction of plant and animal species. And we are all threatened by climate change. Fortunately, more and more people have gradually become aware of the terrible harm we have inflicted on Planet Earth and that 'ecocide' – the destruction of the environment – is a crime. And, let's face it, it is not only a crime against nature, but also against humanity, particularly against future generations.

I have spent a great deal of my life in the rainforest and other wilderness areas, and I have acquired an understanding of the interconnectedness of living things, the fact that each species of plant and animal has a role to play in the amazing tapestry of life. We must understand that we humans are part of the natural world, not separate from it. That we are utterly dependent on Mother Nature, and when we destroy her, we are also ultimately threatening our own species with extinction. For we are, in the end, just one species among many – though unfortunately the most destructive that has ever evolved.

The word 'ecocide' has a similar ring to 'genocide' – the mass killing of one ethnic group by another. And 'ecocide' does indeed imply the mass killing of the natural world, the diversity of species within an ecosystem. Like genocide, ecocide generates feelings of shock, horror – and anger. It helps people to understand that our onslaught against nature is truly an atrocity.

Ecocide, ethically and morally, is a crime. How can it be right for one species among many to destroy other species and the ecosystems that support them? And it is ethically and morally a crime against humanity. Listing ecocide as a crime at the International Criminal Court will help to protect Mother Nature and support those who are working to save her. And that number is growing around the world, as more and more people begin to make ethical choices in the way they live their lives, as corporations begin to change their harmful practices, and as young people increasingly take action to advocate for and work for a more sustainable way of life.

Polly Higgins called upon us to 'dare to be great'. And I echo that when I tell people that each one of us has an indomitable spirit and that we must work to grow it and fight to make the world a better place for all life. Polly's sheer tenacity and perseverance in her fight for ecocide to be recognised as the crime that it is has paid off, as it seems truly possible that this law will finally be put in place.

Let us hope it will be in time.

Dame Jane Goodall
February 2020

FORWARD

by Michael Mansfield QC

According to convention this section is called an afterword, but I have an idea that Polly would have preferred a 'forward' ... it encapsulates the essence of this book, her life force and her trajectory – like the far-reaching 'ripple effect', whereby she was forever stirring the often still waters of the human conscience with a gentle but increasingly penetrating persuasion on behalf of her client 'the Earth'.

As a fellow lawyer it was this simple but radicalising concept that captured my imagination from the moment I met her, over fifteen years ago. So accustomed to representing people, the thought that our planet was a living organism that needed defending brought the whole struggle to life.

The steady ripple we both worked on was 'Stop Ecocide'. Steadfastly supported by her husband Ian, himself a lawyer, Polly lighted upon a grand design: a mock trial in the newly furbished UK Supreme Court in 2011 for the world to see how, in practical terms, ecocide as a fifth 'crime against peace' alongside genocide might work. It was streamed live (still available on YouTube) and was an astounding success. Thereafter it contributed to her global efforts with governments to add this offence to the Rome Statute. Bear in mind ecocide was originally intended to be included in the Statute but opposition, obstruction and obfuscation by (among others) the USA and the UK ensured it was kept off the international criminal agenda.

Since then, and ironically since her untimely death last spring, the gathering impact of her perpetual stirring has surfaced on a global wave of awareness, anger and action. The Extinction Rebellion movement and powerful protests by striking schoolchildren have propelled the immediate risks to the integrity of our planet to the forefront. Prominent banners proclaim the iniquity of 'climate crime' – exactly the message Polly had so carefully articulated.

In the autumn of 2019 at the International Criminal Court in The Hague (where 'crimes against peace' are tried), Polly's ripple effect emerged in an initiative by island states threatened by rising sea levels and cyclones. The Vanuatan ambassador called for serious discussion of an amendment to the Rome Statute to finally include 'ecocide'. Supported shortly afterward by the Maldives, this was the first time since the Statute was created in 1998 that a nation state had taken this step. A two-thirds majority of the 123 member states could see this through ... we must maintain the pressure.

One would have thought the various catastrophes last year alone – exemplified by extensive fires across Africa, South America and Australia – would by now have moved all hearts and minds to the realisation that 'climate and ecological crisis' is no understatement. Indeed, it is already too late for some.

However, there are now wider signs of awakening: fast food chains, culinary and health experts and major food stores all eager to supply and endorse vegan products; the vehicle and aviation industry desperately attempting to be seen as compliant with climate targets; and recently, questions emerging around 5G/6G technologies and AI.

Here in the UK, due to hosting the next round of COP talks in Glasgow later this year, the government will at last be forced to pay regard and respect to environmental issues. And hard on the heels of Glasgow will be the International Criminal Court's annual assembly in New York, where international state level diplomacy has the opportunity to step up another gear.

It's time to vigorously stir the waters once more, with the thunder of the youthful Greta Thunberg and the lifelong persistence and courage displayed by Polly Higgins.

Michael Mansfield QC
February 2020

APPENDIX 1

ECOCIDE LAW TIMELINE

1985–96	Ecocide discussed as part of the preliminary drafting of what was to become the Rome Statute of the International Criminal Court (ICC).
1996	Despite support from many countries, ecocide is dropped from the drafting for undisclosed reasons.
1998	The Rome Statute is finalised with jurisdiction over three crimes, described as 'most serious crimes of concern to the international community as a whole': Genocide, Crimes Against Humanity and War Crimes (which has a limited provision for intentional environmental damage during wartime only); countries begin to ratify.
2002	The International Criminal Court (ICC) is established.

2010	The amendment of the Crime of Aggression is adopted into the Statute, but not prosecutable by the ICC until thirty-plus member states ratify and enforce.
	Polly Higgins presents a definition of ecocide to the UN's International Law Commission: Ecocide is loss, damage or destruction of ecosystem(s) of a given territory, whether by human agency or by other causes, to such an extent that peaceful enjoyment by the inhabitants of that territory has been or will be severely diminished.
2011	A mock trial is held in the UK Supreme Court using Polly's draft Ecocide Act with Michael Mansfield QC prosecuting. Ecocide is shown to be a viable, triable crime in the context of UK law.
2012–16	Polly seeds the concept of replacing the 'missing law' of ecocide into the Rome Statute, engaging with a wide range of audiences and forums worldwide from government to grassroots, NGOs to influencers. She inspires thousands, from lawyers to activist groups, and builds a global following. All world governments are notified of the possibility of adding ecocide to the Rome Statute.

2015	Following their significant role in negotiations for the Paris Agreement, Polly recognises the potential importance of a Law of Ecocide for Small Island Developing States at the frontlines of climate change and begins to make contact with these vulnerable countries.
2016	The first state to make contact with Polly is Vanuatu, a leading voice among Pacific Island nations. Polly and a small advisory team accompany Vanuatan delegates to the ICC's annual assembly.
	Repeatedly disappointed by the failure of environmental foundations and NGOs to support her work, Polly Higgins creates the Earth Protectors Trust Fund with a view to crowdfunding support for climate-vulnerable states to progress Ecocide Law.
	In an unprecedented move, Polly has the Trust Fund document apostilled (legally validated) in virtually every jurisdiction in the world, thereby giving it evidential weight in courts of law across the globe. The intention is to provide those on the frontlines of ecocide who sign the document with primary evidence that they are taking action to prevent harm, not to cause it – i.e. they are not criminals, but what Polly later termed 'Conscientious Protectors'.

2017	With eco-activist and close colleague Jojo Mehta, Polly co-founds non-profit Ecological Defence Integrity (EDI) to continue the diplomatic and legal advocacy work.
	Together they launch a public-facing campaign to crowdfund EDI's work; initially called Mission LifeForce, this campaign was later renamed Stop Ecocide. Supporters declare themselves Earth Protectors and gift into the globally validated Earth Protectors Trust Fund. Funds are ring-fenced to directly support climate vulnerable states, such as Vanuatu, and progress the law at the international level.
	The campaign raises enough funds to send Polly and a team of lawyers and researchers to the ICC's assembly in New York to meet representatives from these states.
2018	The campaign begins to grow.
	A number of 'Conscientious Protectors' use the founding document in the UK courts to notable effect – they are given unusual leeway to express their motivations and call witnesses. Fines given are minimal.
July 2018	Jurisdiction of the ICC over Crime of Aggression amendment activated.
October 2018	Extinction Rebellion launched in the UK. ('Conscientious Protector' armbands used by rebels.)

December 2018	Polly makes the bold move, at a special event held alongside the ICC's assembly in The Hague, of highlighting suspects for a potential crime of 'Climate Ecocide', naming two CEOs of Shell and a Dutch minister. The press is wary of publishing on the subject – pressure behind the scenes is suspected.
2019	A persistent cluster of chest infections is revealed to have far more serious implications – Polly has a rapidly spreading lung cancer.
21 March 2019	Polly is told she has 6 weeks to live.
April 2019	The campaign to establish Ecocide Law rebrands as Stop Ecocide.
15 April 2019	Rebel action at Shell's London HQ is dedicated to Polly. Rebellion week is peppered with Stop Ecocide placards.
21 April 2019	Easter Day: Polly dies. Her passing is announced on the Rebellion stage in London just before Greta Thunberg addresses the crowd.
May 2019	Polly's funeral is attended by many hundreds. She is buried in the grounds of Holy Trinity Church, Slad.
	Following Polly's death, the campaign experiences a powerful upsurge in support and volunteering. Director and co-founder Jojo Mehta coordinates the growing team, becoming key spokesperson for the campaign and the international advocacy work.

| November 2019 | Pope Francis, addressing the International Association of Penal Law (AIDP) calls on the international community to recognise ecocide as a 'fifth category of crimes against peace'. |
| December 2019 | In their official statements at the ICC's annual assembly, two sovereign states (Vanuatu and the Maldives) call for serious consideration of the addition of a crime of ecocide to the Rome Statute. |

WHAT'S HAPPENING NOW: CREATING A MORAL MANDATE TO PROTECT LIFE ON EARTH

We believe, as Polly did, that the most effective way to prevent further devastation is to **make ecocide an international crime** – and we are actively helping to make this happen.

A crime of ecocide has great power to change corporate behaviour by holding the CEOs of the world's biggest polluting companies and government ministers individually responsible for ecocides they cause or permit. It provides a real deterrent. Even *talking* about destroying nature as a *crime* begins to change the global conversation. We universally consider it unacceptable to kill people but often forget that we – and all of human society and culture – are fundamentally dependent upon and part of the wider ecosystems of the Earth. Once we start thinking and talking about mass destruction of nature as equivalent to mass destruction of people, we start to connect those dots. Corporations must consider how to *legitimately* make money (right now that means, for example, without killing people).

Unlike international climate negotiations, such as the COP (UN Conference of the Parties) talks where the wealthiest nations and corporations lobby for resolutions to suit them, at the International Criminal Court (ICC) climate- and ecocide-vulnerable states have an equal voice with the bigger players. This means that those on the frontline of the climate and ecological emergency have the opportunity to take action into their own hands and seek justice. Their combined voices can initiate an ecocide amendment – and even carry it through. That is hugely exciting.

As the Law of Ecocide becomes visible on the horizon, banks and insurers will have to reconsider what they finance and underwrite; CEOs will have to think about whether they want to be seen or talked about in the same bracket as war criminals. It stimulates a new kind of innovation that is crucial to protecting the Earth's ability to function and initiates a much-needed transition period – away from harmful industrial and extractive activities to a more regenerative approach. It is a transition that civil society all over the world is starting to demand with a louder and louder voice. Ecocide Law will be required – sooner or later – if we wish to survive and thrive on Earth.

2019 was a turning point. The hard work that so many dedicated activists have been engaging in for decades on behalf of nature is finally becoming visible. More and more people are using the term 'ecocide' because it is now impossible to ignore our failure to prevent the widespread and systematic destruction of ecosystems. The word literally means 'to destroy one's home' – the ecosystems we depend upon.

The term was taken to the streets by Extinction Rebellion and the Youth Climate Strikers inspired by Greta Thunberg. The French government twice considered legislating for ecocide. Even the Pope called for ecocide to be recognised as a crime against peace under the Rome Statute (the governing document of the ICC), exactly as we have been campaigning for and using the same language and definitions as Polly put forward to the UN Law Commission. And most significantly, the conversation has now moved up to international state level, as the governments of two nations (Vanuatu and the Maldives) officially called for the Assembly of the ICC to seriously consider amending the Rome Statute to include ecocide.

Ecological Defence Integrity (EDI), the NGO Polly Higgins co-founded with Jojo Mehta, now has a core team of lawyers, academics, researchers and diplomatic contacts working towards the establishment of an international crime of ecocide. We also have a growing international communications and outreach team taking forward the Stop Ecocide campaign, supported by dozens of volunteers. Thousands of supporters have become self-declared 'Earth Protectors', contributing funds to the work, which has three key elements:

Diplomatic/legal – EDI's international team is working with climate- and ecocide-vulnerable states which have the power to propose an ecocide amendment to the Rome

Statute. The ICC's annual assembly in December is the key forum for advancing this work. We have accompanied Small Island ('Great Ocean') Developing State representatives and helped amplify their voices and concerns there for four consecutive years, as the nations most impacted by the climate emergency.

Campaigning – Our public-facing Stop Ecocide campaign is both funding this work and raising global awareness of Ecocide Law as a viable way of addressing our global crisis. Supporters declare themselves Earth Protectors and contribute to a globally validated Trust Fund which is ringfenced to support the diplomatic/legal work.

Movement Building – A pilot scheme for Earth Protector Communities is already under way, seeding a global collaborative movement in which towns, schools and colleges, businesses and other institutions work together to protect land, wildlife, air, soil and water, as well as endorsing the Stop Ecocide campaign. The Regenerative Community Toolkit, a powerful conceptual and practical resource for Earth Protector Communities of all types and sizes, is due to launch in 2020 and is directly inspired by this book.

For legal/historical information, visit:
www.EcocideLaw.com
For the latest on the campaign and to add your support, visit:
www.StopEcocide.earth
For the latest on Earth Protector Communities, visit:
www.EarthProtectorCommunities.net

WHAT YOU CAN DO: BECOME AN EARTH PROTECTOR

Anyone can directly support our international legal and diplomatic work by signing up as an Earth Protector on our website www.StopEcocide.earth. As an Earth Protector, you become an active part of a global movement bringing in a people's law to protect the Earth. You become a signatory to the campaign's founding document (the Earth Protectors Trust Fund document), which states:

> Becoming a trustee of this document is to become an Earth Protector and Trustee of the Earth. It is a declaration of love and acknowledgement that the Earth, the ecosystems of Earth and inhabitants of Earth whether human or otherwise have the right to peaceful enjoyment. It is a declaration of belief that this peaceful enjoyment is both a moral and legal right, and

that any human act or omission which severely diminishes such peaceful enjoyment is a crime.

Becoming a Trustee of the Earth is to become a protector of a law which is in alignment with a universally recognised moral code of respect, peace and a duty of care for all life. It is a direct expression of intent to create peace between all beings.

Becoming an Earth Protector also supports you if you are taking peaceful direct action as a 'Conscientious Protector'. You have the human right to assert your freedom of conscience under Article 9 of the European Convention of Human Rights or Article 18 of the Universal Declaration of Human Rights. This becomes useful if you are likely to face arrest as a result of acting from your conscience to prevent ecocide. Signing up as an Earth Protector gives you a way to bring your activism into the courtroom – it is primary evidence that you are acting to prevent harm, not to cause it.

Find out more at:
www.stopecocide.earth/conscientious-protectors

And talk about it!

Spread the word in your networks and be part of changing the rules – the key thing is *making visible and understood* that Ecocide Law is simple, transformational and, above all, possible. It creates hope and a powerful and positive way forward for all of us. There are plenty of materials on our websites to help do this, and more in the pipeline ... because we can all dare to be great.

APPENDIX 4

ECOCIDE LAW

Ecocide is the extensive damage to, destruction of or loss of ecosystem(s) of a given territory, whether by human agency or by other causes, to such an extent that peaceful enjoyment by the inhabitants of that territory has been or will be severely diminished.

Definition submitted to the UN Law Commission
by Polly Higgins, 2010[13]

The purpose for creating the offence of ecocide as the 5th International Crime Against Peace is to put in place at the very top level an international law. As of April 2020, 123 nations are signatories of the Rome Statute. International Crime (which is codified in the Rome Statute) applies not only to the signatory states. If and when a person commits a Crime Against Peace, the International Criminal Court has powers to intervene in certain circumstances, even if the person or state involved is a non-signatory. The Rome Statute is one of the most powerful documents in the world, assigning 'the most serious crimes of concern to the international community as a whole'[14] over and above all other laws. In addition, primary legislation to be used at a national level has also been drafted by Polly Higgins, called the Ecocide Act (visit: www.ecocidelaw. com). Section 6 of the Ecocide Act sets out the explicit right that is given recognition by the crime of ecocide:

6. The right to life is a universal right and where a person, company organisation, partnership, or any other legal entity causes extensive damage to, destruction of or loss of human and or non-human life of the inhabitants of a territory ... is guilty of the crime of ecocide.

Crimes that already exist within the jurisdiction of the International Criminal Court under Article 5 of the Rome Statute are known collectively as Crimes Against Peace.

They are:

Article 5(1) The jurisdiction of the Court shall be limited to the most serious crimes of concern to the international community as a whole. The Court has jurisdiction in accordance with this Statute with respect to the following crimes:
The Crime of Genocide;
Crimes Against Humanity;
War Crimes;
The Crime of Aggression.
To be added:
The Crime of Ecocide.

The inclusion of Ecocide Law as international law prohibits mass damage and destruction of the Earth and, as defined above, creates a legal duty of care for all inhabitants that have been or are at risk of being significantly harmed due to ecocide. The duty of care applies to prevent, prohibit and pre-empt both human-caused ecocide and natural catastrophes. Where ecocide occurs as a crime, remedy can be sought through national courts and the International Criminal Court (ICC) or a similar body. Proposals for a new court exist, such as The Brussels Charter[15] and the Coalition for the International Court for the Environment.[16] Ecocide Law has both criminal and civil law application.

A Law of Ecocide:

prevents the risk of and/or actual extensive damage to, destruction of or loss of ecosystem(s);

prohibits decisions that result in extensive damage to or destruction of or loss of ecosystem(s);

pre-empts decision-making of a political, financial and business nature that may lead to significant harm.

Ecocide Law Duty of Care

superior responsibility provision: an international and transboundary duty of care on any person or persons who exercises a position of superior responsibility, without exemption, in either private or public capacity to prevent the risk of and/or actual extensive damage to or destruction of or loss of ecosystem(s).

business provision: an international and transboundary duty of care on CEOs and directors of a business and/or any person who exercises rights over a given territory to ensure ecocide does not occur.

political provision: an international and transboundary duty of care on governmental actors, specifically Heads of State and Ministers with environment/energy/climate change portfolios, to ensure ecocide does not occur and to provide emergency assistance before, during and after to other territories at risk or adversely affected by ecocide.

financial provision: an international and transboundary duty of care on financiers, investors, CEOs and directors of any banking and investment institution who exercises a position of superior responsibility, to ensure ecocide is not financed.

A Crime of Ecocide:

prohibits damage, destruction and loss of ecosystems over a certain size, duration or impact; creates consequence-based law (prohibition of hazard), not just risk abatement;

sets in place a mandatory provision of shared nation responsibility for supporting aid and assistance to ecocide-affected territories;

halts the flow of daily destruction that occurs during peacetime at a level that is already defined as criminal activity in war-time;

shifts the burden of responsibility to those in a position of 'superior responsibility';

imposes an overriding pre-emptive legal duty on all corporations, banks and investment to prevent business from profiteering out of activity that causes mass damage, destruction or loss of ecosystems;

imposes an overriding primary legal obligation on all governments to prohibit investment and policy that causes or supports ecocide.

Trusteeship

A Law of Ecocide also imputes a legal duty of care in the event of natural catastrophe (e.g. rising sea levels, droughts, earthquakes). The United Nations Trusteeship Council's purpose (as one of the founding pillars of the UN Charter) was to assist territories that were unable to self-govern; it is proposed that the Trusteeship Council re-open its doors and be put to use again to assist non self-governing territories that have been or are at risk of being harmed by ecocide.[17]

It can be used to assist territories suffering from Ecological Ecocide as well as Cultural Ecocide.

By re-opening the UN Trusteeship Council chamber (closed in 1994). Member states have a ready-made forum in which to determine what support and aid to put in place for non-self-governing territories facing ecocide.

Damage to or destruction of or loss of ecosystem(s) leads to:

~ crimes against humanity, nature and future generations;

~ conflict;

~ diminution in quality of life for all inhabitants in the territory affected;

~ diminution of health and wellbeing for all inhabitants;

~ catastrophic disasters leading to food loss, poverty, water pollution and shortages, unnatural climate change, deforestation and more.

Ecocide Law creates an international and transboundary duty of care which is preventative, pre-emptive and prohibitive in nature ('First do no harm' principle). Ecocide Law breaks cycles of harm.

For more background and historical information, see: **www.EcocideLaw.com**

ENDNOTES

1. See Appendix 4: Ecocide Law for more detail.
2. See School of Advanced Study, University of London, Human Rights Consortium's Ecocide Project at hrc.sas.ac.uk/research-themes/environmental-justice/ecocide-project and their research paper: *Ecocide is the Missing 5th Crime Against Peace* (Dr Damien Short (ed.), London, updated 2013. Available at: sas-space.sas.ac.uk/4830/1/Ecocide_research_report_19_July_13.pdf).
3. Polly Higgins, *Eradicating Ecocide: Laws and Governance to Prevent the Destruction of Our Planet* (London, 2010) and *Earth is Our Business: Changing the Rules of the Game* (London, 2012).
4. See Useful Documents page at: ecocidelaw.com/resources/documents/.
5. Economy = Greek *oikonomia* 'household management', based on *oikos* 'house' + *nemein* 'manage'.
6. See Schumann's Resonance. In 1954, Prof. Schumann discovered that Earth's electromagnetic pulse is 7.83 Hz (known in humans as theta wave). His successor Dr Konig proposed we 'tune into' the Earth when we resonate at 7.8 Hz.

7. Michel Foucault, *Techniques of Parrhesia* (Berkeley University, 1983). See: foucault.info/parrhesia/foucault.DT5. techniquesParrhesia.en/.

8. See the Hoffmann Institute in US (hoffmaninstitute.org) and UK (hoffmaninstitute.co.uk); also operating in many countries throughout the world.

9. Rob Hopkins, *Transition Handbook: From Oil Dependency to Local Resilience* (Cambridge, 2008).

10. Polly Higgins, *Eradicating Ecocide*, pp. XV, 5, 6 and 150.

11. Thich Nhat Hanh – a renowned Zen master, a poet, and a peace activist – is the author of many books including *True Love: A Practice for Awakening the Heart* (Colorado, 2006).

12. Simon Sinek, *Start With Why* (London, 2009), see also his TED talk: www.youtube.com/watch?v=sioZd3AxmnE.

13. Polly Higgins, *Eradicating Ecocide: laws and governance to prevent the destruction of our planet* (London, 2010), pp. 61– 92.

14. Preamble, Rome Statute.

15. See: www.endecocide.org/en/charter-of-brussels/.

16. See: www.icecoalition.com and see also the International Court for the Environment Foundation.

17. See Chapter 6, Polly Higgins, *Eradicating Ecocide*, pp. 72–92.

ABOUT THIS BOOK

What you are holding in your hands is a gift. It is also an invitation to you to help spread my quest. You can do this in a number of ways: you can gift this book to others, ask your local bookshop to stock it and give it a display in their window. Please be a bridge in any way you think can help. Take it to others in your community, seed it into book clubs, libraries, give it a write-up and post it onto independent, local and community sites, send it to magazines and press.

Stand up and speak about daring to be great, join one of the growing online communities who are engaging with Ecocide Law (see Stop Ecocide: www.stopecocide.earth) or become an Earth Protector.

Ultimately, the purpose of this book is to seed greatness and Ecocide Law right across the world. If this book has made your heart sing, then I invite you to gift some of your time, energy and/or money – all of which are equally valued.

From one heart to another,

Polly Higgins
November 2014

MORE ABOUT POLLY

Polly's life and work were a beacon for so many people, as she devoted all her time and unquenchable spirit to one client – the Earth. She spent the last decade making the word 'ecocide' globally understood by giving talks, making documentaries and advising governments. Along the way she inspired thousands, from parliamentarians to ecologists and from lawyers to artists.

She was born in Glasgow and went on to study a degree in cultural history at Aberdeen University, a diploma in semiology at Utrecht University and a postgraduate degree in fine and decorative arts from Glasgow University. She funded her way through bar school by setting up her own catering business and was called to the English bar in 1998. She began her career as a barrister, but when she posed herself the question of what it would take to create a legal duty of care for the Earth, she left the UK courtroom behind and set out on a journey that would see her become a world-renowned Ecocide Law expert.

Polly was named one of the World's Top 10 Visionary Thinkers by the *Ecologist* and was celebrated as The Planet's Lawyer by the 2010 Change Awards. Her first book, *Eradicating Ecocide*, won the People's Book Prize in 2011. Amongst many of her keynote speeches, she delivered the 2012 50th anniversary Rachel Carson Memorial Lecture in London and the Netherlands. Polly continued to garner international acclaim and a number of awards for her work advocating for a Law of Ecocide. She received an Honoris Causa Doctorate from Business School Lausanne 2013; in the same year she became the Honorary Arne Naess Professor at Oslo University. In November 2015, the Dutch broadcaster VPRO featured a documentary about her work, called *Advocate for the Earth*. She was ranked as No.35 in *Salt* magazine's 2016 Top 100 Inspiring Women of the world list, was the 2016 recipient of Polarbröd's Utstickarpriset for Future Leadership, and the 2017 prizewinner of the Slovakian Ekotopfilm Award.

She often spoke of drawing strength from being rooted in the Stroud Valleys, which she moved to with her husband Ian, and her love of the land was a strong nurturing force in her life and work.

Polly was diagnosed with an aggressive form of cancer in 2019, and passed away on 21 April 2019, aged 50. She was passionate that her life's work would be continued by the incredible team she had built around her: 'My legal team will continue undeterred,' she said.

Her advocacy work is continued by Ecological Defence Integrity (EDI), the NGO she co-founded, and her empowering spirit is embodied in the Stop Ecocide and Earth Protector campaigns that she passionately believed would create the better future we all need:

There are millions who care so much and feel so powerless about the future, and I would love to see them begin to understand the power of this one, simple law to protect the Earth – to realise it's possible, even straightforward. I wish I could live to see a million Earth Protectors standing for it – because I believe they will.

ACKNOWLEDGEMENTS

Like so many things to do with Polly, this book has come together in extraordinary ways. From an initial chat at the Stop Ecocide stand at the Hawkwood Seed Festival in Stroud between Anita van Rossum, the campaign's Head of Outreach, and Chloé Dyson (then a hopeful volunteer) the idea was taken to London and picked up by Clive Wilson, Head of Books at TCO London. It boomeranged straight back to Gloucestershire and connected with Jo de Vries, the consultant commissioning editor for The History Press's newly formed non-fiction imprint Flint, who just happened to be looking for people and books that could 'spark conversation'. As Jo so beautifully put it: 'It's so strange how all these connections intertwine, or rather, it's exactly as Polly says: you open yourself up to a different path, and you start to attract like-minded people like a magnet.'

We are incredibly grateful to the whole team at The History Press and Flint, including Laura Perehinec, Gareth Swain, Jamie Kinnear, Katie Beard, Ian Pearson, Jezz Palmer, Fenton Coulthurst, Jessica Gofton, Caitlin Kirkman, Molly Evans, Jonathon Harris and Tracey Moore. They have moved mountains in the publishing world and really lived up to the title of the book to make sure we could release this new edition in less than six months, in time for the anniversary of Polly's passing. Thank you to Jo de Vries, in particular, who immediately recognised the potential in Polly's words. You have done them justice in the edit of the text, held the project from beginning to end, been so generous with your energy and time – with the sole purpose of getting the message out to as many people as possible – all the while being an absolute joy to work with.

We also have to thank:

Joe Magee for his beautiful cover illustration evoking Polly's belief in the importance of being rooted in order to rise up, and her faith in humanity and love to heal nature.
Lupe de la Vallina for generously supplying the photograph of Polly.
Anita van Rossum for championing the reprint of the book, inspired by dozens of 'Polly-nators' from all over the world who kept requesting copies of *I Dare You To Be Great*, encouraging us to embark on this quest.

Chloé Dyson, now Press Officer at Stop Ecocide, for being the connector and helping to bring the book back into circulation, as well as the wider team at Stop Ecocide who have supported the project in so many ways.

Jojo Mehta for access to the original text, and for your invaluable insight and unwavering support throughout. You made this possible.

And **Polly Higgins**, for writing this book and continuing to inspire us in truly extraordinary ways.

The Great Work continues.
It's now in your hands.

DARE

TO BE

GREAT